THE BREEDING BIRDS OF EUROPE: A PHOTOGRAPHIC HANDBOOK

The Breeding Birds of Europe 1

A PHOTOGRAPHIC HANDBOOK

Divers to Auks

Manfred Pforr and Alfred Limbrunner

Translated by Richard Stoneman
Edited by Iain Robertson

CROOM HELM LONDON

© 1981 Croom Helm
Croom Helm Ltd, 2 – 10 St John's Road, London SW 11
ISBN 0-7099-2013-X

Layout: Manfred Pforr, who also supplied the drawings for
the general section and for the distribution maps.
Preparation of text was shared by Alfred Limbrunner
(87 species, 8 families) and Manfred Pforr (70 species,
3 families).

Colour lithography by H. Jahn KG, Bielefeld.
Printed by Heinrich Silber, Niestetal-Heiligenrode,
West-Germany.
Bound by Freitag & Co., Kassel, West-Germany.

Introduction

Among the many books on birds there are only a few which are illustrated entirely by colour photographs, and still fewer that portray both adult birds and their nests and eggs: this is the purpose of this book.

Where both sexes could be shown together or where sexes are alike, photographs showing non-breeding plumage or flight shots have been included. There were, of course, difficulties in the case of rarer species where photographs were hard to obtain.

Unfortunately some species have had to be treated summarily and a few omitted altogether, these are listed on page 335. Because of the disturbance factor involved the photographers were unable to obtain photographs of the eggs of some hole-nesting species. However, as most of these species lay white eggs, the size indication in the tables is sufficient for identification.

Where records were available the place and date of the photograph were added to the abbreviated name of the photographer in the captions.

The text does not attempt to deal with identification, which is well covered in other works. Instead the information given is concerned with habitat, food, breeding biology and migration. Key information on each species is presented in the form of tables and there is a distribution map showing the European breeding range. Size and weight have been averaged out because of the considerable variation within some species. Egg size may also vary considerably. There are problems in reproducing bird calls in phonetic form due to the varied interpretation of the sounds by different observers. The descriptions given here are therefore our own impressions.

Different races or colour-phases of the same species are illustrated where suitable photographs were available.

The populations of many European birds are endangered through the destruction of habitat for agriculture or urban development, through the use of pesticides and intensive agricultural methods, through tourism and disturbance. The most severely endangered species are listed in the 'red lists' of the International Council for the Protection of Birds, based on the 'Red Data Books' of the International Union for Conservation of Nature (IUCN). These lists are under constant revision in different countries where changes in status are recorded. If attention is paid to

the requirements of certain species and
protection afforded to them recolonisation
or a recovery in numbers may result. The bird-
watcher should behave responsibly towards
all wildlife, whether endangered or not.
It should be stressed that the photographs of
endangered species included in the book
were either obtained at a time when the
danger was not recognised or by taking the
greatest care to avoid disturbance which might
affect the success of the nest.
We would like to thank Max Kasparek, who
supported us with his professional advice
and editorial co-operation, and all the
photographers without whose readiness to
collaborate this book could never have been
published in such a complete form.

Contents

Contents

General Section
The Breeding Birds of Europe

Divers (Order Gaviiformes)

Although similar in many respects, the two groups, divers and grebes, are not closely related, divers having affinities with Charadriiformes. Divers comprise only one family, Gaviidae, containing four species. Their distribution is circumpolar, occupying an ecological niche similar to that of grebes in northern latitudes.

They breed on fresh water where they obtain their food, but birds nesting near the coast will obtain their food in the sea during the breeding season. In winter all species are predominantly maritime in Europe.

Divers are so adapted to an aquatic environment that their legs are set too far back to enable them to walk on or take off from land. Their nests, which are always solitary, are sited on land within shuffling distance of the water's edge. When diving they make use of their laterally flattened legs as well as swimming with half-opened wings. Like grebes, divers have a distinct breeding plumage quite different from their drab non-breeding plumage.

Sexes have similar plumage and vary only slightly in size, the ♂♂ being somewhat larger.

All four species visit Britain in winter, though the White-billed Diver is a vagrant. Two species breed regularly and the Great Northern Diver occasionally summers in Britain and has bred here, though it normally only breeds in Iceland in its European range.

Divers normally lay two olive-brown eggs, marked with darker spots. Their young differ from those of grebes, being drab and unmarked in juvenile plumage. Like all diving birds, they are dependant on their parents for a relatively long time.

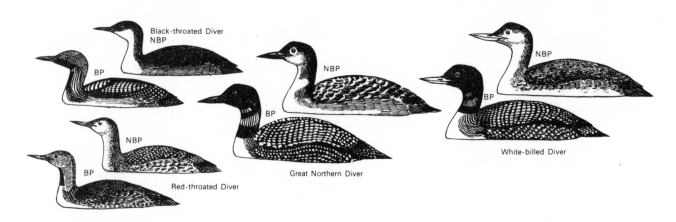

Black-throated Diver NBP
BP
NBP
BP
Red-throated Diver
BP
NBP
Great Northern Diver
NBP
BP
White-billed Diver

Grebes (Order Podicipediformes)

The general similarity of grebes to divers is due to convergent evolution rather than any close relationship. There is only one family, Podicipedidae, containing seven genera, two of which, Tachybaptus and Podiceps, contain the five European breeding species.

Grebes are typical inhabitants of inland waters and, like divers, they are specialised for an aquatic life and experience difficulty in walking on or taking off from land.

Grebes have a distinct breeding plumage characterised by the presence of crests in the four Podiceps species. In non-breeding plumage they are mainly black, grey and white.

Grebes have impressive courtship rituals in which both partners participate. There is no sexual dimorphism and sexes differ only slightly in size, the ♂♂ being the larger.

When swimming underwater only the feet are used, the wings being partially covered by the protective down of the flanks. Unlike divers, they often breed colonially. They construct nests of rotting water-plants usually in emergent vegetation. The eggs are white at first but quickly become stained and discoloured through contact with the nesting material. Young grebes have distinctive juvenile plumages, markedly striped according to species.

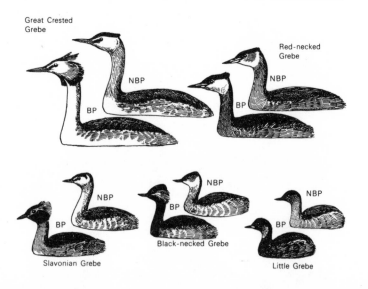

Great Crested Grebe
NBP
BP
Red-necked Grebe
NBP
BP
NBP
BP
Slavonian Grebe
NBP
BP
Black-necked Grebe
NBP
BP
Little Grebe

Petrels and Shearwaters
(Order Procellariiformes)

This order is also known as 'tube-noses', so called because of the two tubular nostrils present on the top of the bill. The Order contains small, Swift-sized birds as well as the giant Albatrosses (the largest flying birds in the world) in four families. The European representatives are contained in two families, Shearwaters, Petrels and Fulmars in Procellariidae and Storm Petrels in Hydrobatidae. There are three species in the former family, each in a different genus, and two in the latter, also in different genera.

All are superb fliers, adapted to ocean-wandering. They feed principally on marine organisms. Apart from the Fulmar, they only visit land during the breeding season and then only at night. They often nest in dense colonies, usually on offshore islands. They have concealed nests in burrows or rock-crevices, though Fulmars breed in open sites: all lay a single, white egg. A character of the Order is the presence of stomach-oil, an evil-smelling liquid derived from dietary residue. This is used to feed small chicks and is also squirted at intruders in territorial defence. All species have a musty odour which permeates their nesting areas.

The Procellariidae are mainly grey or brownish above and white below, with a characteristic gliding flight. The Hydrobatidae are mainly black with pale rumps and wing panels and have a weaker flight. Both groups are very vocal during the breeding season, particularly those that visit their colonies after dark. The young are covered in grey or white down, vestiges of which may remain at fledging time.

Cory's Shearwater

Fulmar

Light phase

Dark phase

Manx Shearwater

Leach's Petrel

Storm Petrel

Gannets, Cormorants and Pelicans (Order Pelecaniformes)

Birds in this order are unique in having all four toes connected by webs (totipalmate). These medium- to large-sized water birds are divided into six families of which three, Sulidae, Phalacrocoracidae and Pelecanidae, are represented in Europe by six breeding species. They are excellent fliers, adapted to an aquatic environment and are rather clumsy on land. The three genera have distinct methods of feeding: Gannets plunge-dive, Cormorants are underwater feeders and Pelicans are social feeders using a scooping technique.

The order includes plumage types from almost pure white to nearly black, the latter confined to the Phalacrocoracidae, which have distinct breeding plumages. There is no sexual dimorphism.

All species are colonial breeders, nesting in trees, in reeds or on the ground, including seacliffs. They generally build nests, though this is not always so. The eggs are white or pale blue, becoming stained by nest materials. The young are nidicolous and have white or blackish down.

Pygmy Cormorant

Gannet

Cormorant

Shag

Mainland race

Atlantic race

White Pelican

Dalmatian Pelican

Herons, Storks and Ibises (Order Ciconiiformes)

These are medium- to large-sized, long-legged wading birds, adapted to feeding in water without the need to swim or dive. Of the five families in the order, three are represented in Europe: Herons and Bitterns (Ardeidae), Storks (Ciconiidae) and Ibises and Spoonbill (Threskiornithidae), with thirteen species between them. All live predominantly on small aquatic creatures, though some species will take both vertebrates and invertebrates on land. Herons and Bitterns fly with their necks folded into an 'S' shape, with their heads pulled back, the other species fly with their necks straight out. About half the species have a distinct breeding plumage and one, the Little Bittern, is sexually dimorphic.

Most species normally breed in colonies: their nests are built in trees, on rocks or buildings and in swamp vegetation. Sometimes several species will breed in mixed colonies. The young are nidicolous and, with the exception of Night Heron, there is little difference between immature and adult plumage.

Grey Heron

Purple Heron

Squacco Heron

Night Heron

Great White Egret

Bittern

Little Egret

Little Bittern

Cattle Egret

Spoonbill

Glossy Ibis

Flamingos
(Order Phoenicopteriformes)

These large wading birds are usually placed in one family, Phoenicopteridae, of which one species breeds in Europe. They are intermediate between Ciconiiformes and Anseriformes, though closer to the former. The bill is unique in having large lower and small upper mandibles which are lined with lamellae, thin plates used in filter-feeding. This involves filtering mud and water through the lamellae by the movement of tongue and lower mandible in order to sift out algae and small invertebrates. The Flamingo holds its head upside-down when feeding.

They are exclusively colonial breeders requiring specialised conditions and social stimuli for nesting. The one or two chalky white eggs are laid in the hollow of a conical mound of sunbaked mud scraped up by the parents. The young are covered with whitish down at first, later greyish.

Greater Flamingo

White Stork

Black Stork

12

Ducks and Geese (Order Anseriformes)

This order contains swans, geese and ducks in one family, Anatidae, with thirty-seven species breeding in Europe. The family is sub-divided into Anserini, containing swans and true geese, and seven tribes which contain Shelducks, Perching ducks, Diving ducks, Eiders, Scoters and Sawbills, and Stifftails.

All Anseriformes can fly for long periods and carry their necks stretched out. The plumage is thick and waterproof with an underlying layer of down. The bills show great variation but are generally strong, often compressed laterally with a horny nail at the tip. All species are strictly aquatic, though swans, geese and some duck feed on land. Food consists of fish, all manner of aquatic invertebrates, algae, crustaceans, etc. Species are found on both salt and fresh water with many species becoming maritime outside the breeding season.

Nest-sites are varied: some species use holes in trees, in the ground or among rocks, others nest in open sites. Down is used to cover the eggs. The young are nidifugous and precocial.

Swans and geese show little sexual dimorphism and both sexes take part in parental care. They are essentially vegetarian and often feed on land. Ducks show marked sexual dimorphism in all but a few species. The ♂♂ do not share familial duties. Food is obtained by dabbling or diving in most species, though a few take vegetable matter on land.

Dabbling Ducks

Mallard · Pintail · Gadwall · Wigeon · Marbled Teal · Shoveler · Teal · Garganey · Mandarin Duck

Diving Ducks

Red-crested Pochard · Scaup · Tufted Duck · Pochard · Ferruginous Duck · Goldeneye · Barrow's Goldeneye

Sawbills

Goosander · Red-breasted Merganser · Smew

Shelducks

Shelduck · Ruddy Shelduck

Marine Ducks

Long-tailed Duck ♀ ♂

Harlequin Duck ♀ ♂

Velvet Scoter ♂ ♀

Stifftails

White-headed Duck ♀ ♂

Eider ♂ ♀

King Eider ♂ ♀

Common Scoter ♂ ♀

Geese

Greylag Goose

White-fronted Goose

Lesser White-fronted Goose

Bean Goose

Pink-footed Goose

Canada Goose

Barnacle Goose

Brent Goose

Swans

Mute Swan

Whooper Swan

Bewick's Swan

14

Birds of Prey (Order Falconiformes)

Small to very large diurnal birds of prey. Sharp claws (talons), and a hooked bill are adaptations for feeding or catching prey. They are not related to Owls, which are largely nocturnal. Some species take live prey, others feed only on carrion. Birds of prey are good or superb fliers according to the preferred method of hunting. They may hunt from vantage points like posts or treetops, quarter the land at very varied heights or hunt by stealth in forest habitat.

The nests, known as 'eyries', are generally built in trees, on crags and buildings, or, in some cases, on the ground. Some species use the abandoned nests of other birds. The clutch-size is variable, though always small in the larger species. The young are nidicolous and clad in white down. In immature plumage they often exhibit differences in colour from adult birds. Great differences in size within the Order, and sometimes within species, coupled with variable plumages may make identification difficult.

Birds of prey are found throughout the world with the exception of Antarctica, and there is scarcely a habitat which is not used by at least one species. They are the most severely endangered group of birds, with many species extirpated over much of their former range. Some species are so decimated that individual nests are guarded in an effort to protect the species. Though shooting, nest-destruction, egg-collecting and the taking of young birds for falconry have had a detrimental effect on population, much greater damage has been done by the use of pesticides (to which birds of prey are very susceptible, being at the head of a food-chain) and by destruction of habitat. Despite the protection afforded to birds of prey in many countries there is still a decline in most species.

There are thirty-seven species breeding in Europe, with two families: Hawks, Vultures and Eagles (Accipitridae) and Falcons (Falconidae).

Vultures

Griffon Vulture

Egyptian Vulture

Black Vulture

Lammergeier (Bearded Vulture)

Hawks, Vultures and Eagles
(Family Accipitridae)

This family contains the largest number of species and exhibits a wide variety of adaptive forms. Apart from the Vultures most species feed on living prey, though most will take carrion at times. Food can be collected in the crop until ready to be digested. Feathers, hair, scales and inorganic matter (e.g. bird-rings) are regurgitated in the form of pellets. Bones are usually digested. Many species are migratory: some long-distance migrants cross over the sea at narrows like Gibraltar, the Bosphorus and Falsterbo.

Eagles

Golden Eagle adult

Sea Eagle

Imperial Eagle

Bonelli's Eagle

Spotted Eagle

Short-toed Eagle

Booted Eagle light phase

dark phase

Osprey

Golden Eagle juv.

Pallas's Sea Eagle

Steppe Eagle

Lesser Spotted Eagle

Buzzards

Honey Buzzard

Buzzard

Buzzard (eastern race)

Rough-legged Buzzard

Long-legged Buzzard

Hawks and Sparrow-hawks

Sparrowhawk

Levant Sparrow-hawk

Goshawk

Kites

Red Kite

Black Kite

Black-winged Kite

Harriers

Marsh Harrier ♂ ♀

Hen-Harrier ♂ ♀

Pallid Harrier ♂ ♀

Montagu's Harrier ♂ ♀

Falcons

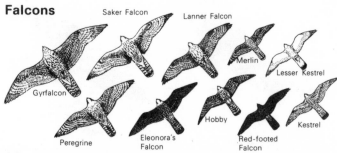

Saker Falcon

Lanner Falcon

Merlin

Lesser Kestrel

Gyrfalcon

Peregrine

Eleonora's Falcon

Hobby

Red-footed Falcon

Kestrel

Falcons (Family Falconidae)

Falcons are distinguished from hawks and their allies by their narrower, pointed wings and by the tooth-like indentation of the upper mandible with corresponding concavities in the lower mandible.

Falcons are fast, agile fliers, generally preying on birds and insects taken in flight. Some species take food from the ground and hover while locating their prey. Some of the larger species will prey on the smaller ones.

Falcons nest on cliffs, in hollow trees and on buildings and in some cases nest on the ground. They do not build nests but take over the nests of other species, particularly Crows.

Grouse, Partridges and Pheasants (Order Galliformes)

This is a very large order containing over 240 species. Fourteen of these breed in Europe and belong to two families, Grouse in Tetraonidae and Pheasants and Partridges in Phasianidae. They are generally stocky birds, adapted for ground-living with strong legs and feet and short, rounded wings. In many species there is a spur above the hind claw, especially in the ♂♂. They can run well and are strong fliers over short distances. Apart from Quail, they are non-migratory, though some are nomadic and others may migrate altitudinally in winter. There is considerable sexual dimorphism in most species with differences in both plumage and size.

Galliformes do not bathe in water but take dust-baths. Most species are polygamous, though some, e.g. Grey Partridge, are strictly monogamous.

Except for the tree-nesting Guans of South America all Galliformes are ground-nesters. The young are nidifugous and precocial, able to fly at an early age, especially in the tree-climbing species.

Summer

♀ ♂

Willow Grouse

Winter

Red Grouse

♀ ♂

Summer

♂

Winter

Ptarmigan

Grouse

♀ Hazel Hen (Hazel Grouse) ♂

♂ Black Grouse

♀

♀

♂

Capercaillie

17

Partridges

Chukar

Rock Partridge

Red-legged Partridge

Barbary Partridge

Partridge

Quail

♂

♀

Pheasant

18

Button-Quails, Cranes, Rails and Bustards (Order Gruiformes)

This order is represented throughout the world with the exception of Antarctica. It is thought to be one of the oldest and can be traced back by at least ten fossil families to the early Tertiary period.

The Order contains a number of differing forms whose relationship is difficult to discern. Basically they are very small to huge ground-living or wading birds, mostly with long necks and long legs. Although many species are primarily aquatic they have not developed webbed feet; only the Coots have indented webs on each toe. There is little or no sexual dimorphism except in certain Rails, and in Bustards, where the ♂♂ have striking plumages.

They are mostly good fliers and some species are migratory, particularly those breeding in northern latitudes. In flight the neck is held outstretched and in Rails the legs dangle. Both sexes share in parental duties except in Bustards, where the ♀♀ brood alone. The young are nidifugous, though less developed than in Galliformes.

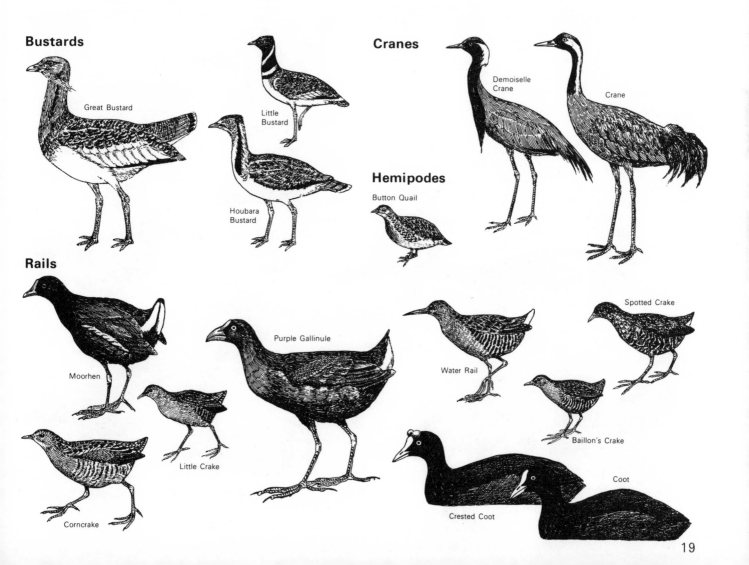

Bustards
Great Bustard
Little Bustard
Houbara Bustard

Cranes
Demoiselle Crane
Crane

Hemipodes
Button Quail

Rails
Moorhen
Little Crake
Corncrake
Purple Gallinule
Water Rail
Spotted Crake
Baillon's Crake
Crested Coot
Coot

Marsh and Shore Birds
(Order Charadriiformes)

Of the sixteen families in this order which is distributed throughout the world, ten breed in Europe. Despite considerable variation in outward appearance they are closely related by similarities of anatomy and behaviour. Their evolution can be traced back over 75 million years and they are most closely related to Crane-like birds.

Their plumage is generally dense and thus suitable for life in an aquatic environment. Dominant colours are grey, brown and white. Many species have a more colourful breeding plumage and this is best developed in the Ruff.

Preferred habitats are seacoasts and margins of freshwater habitats as well as marshes, the draining of which has endangered several species.

Most species have a low reproductive rate, breeding only once a year and laying, at the most, four eggs. The young are well developed soon after hatching and have distinctive juvenile downy plumage. Most species are nidifugous, or nearly so, Auks being an exception. Usually both sexes share brooding and rearing of young, though in snipes the ♀♀ takes this responsibility. In the case of Dotterel and Phalaropes the sex-roles are reversed, with the ♂♂ taking over parental duties. Consequently the ♂♂ have duller plumage than the ♀♀ in the breeding season.

Plovers

Ringed Plover

Kentish Plover

Caspian Plover

Little Ringed Plover

BP

◁ Grey Plover ▷

NBP

NBP

◁ Golden Plover ▷
(northern race)

BP

Dotterel

Turnstone

BP

Golden Plover
(southern race)

Oystercatchers

Oystercatcher

Spur-winged Plover

Lapwing

Sociable Plover

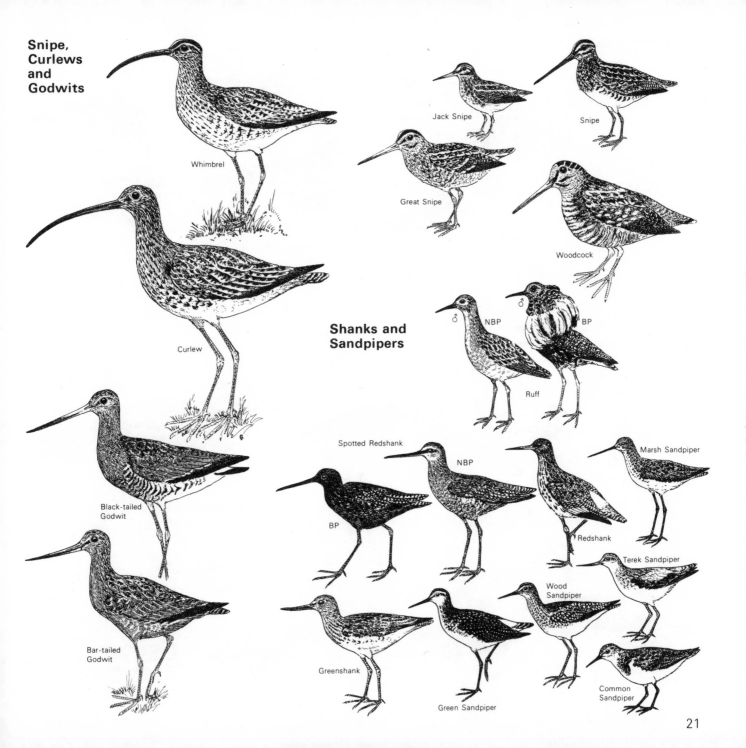

Snipe, Curlews and Godwits

Whimbrel

Curlew

Black-tailed Godwit

Bar-tailed Godwit

Jack Snipe

Snipe

Great Snipe

Woodcock

Shanks and Sandpipers

♂ NBP

♂ BP

Ruff

Spotted Redshank

NBP

Marsh Sandpiper

BP

Redshank

Terek Sandpiper

Greenshank

Green Sandpiper

Wood Sandpiper

Common Sandpiper

21

Stints and Sandpipers

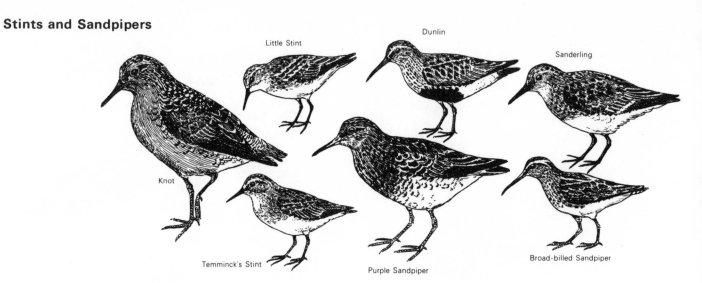

Little Stint

Dunlin

Sanderling

Knot

Temminck's Stint

Purple Sandpiper

Broad-billed Sandpiper

Avocet, Stilt, Stone Curlew, Pratincoles and Phalaropes

Avocet

Black-winged Stilt

Stone Curlew

Collared Pratincole

Black-winged Pratincole

Grey Phalarope

Red-necked Phalarope

Skuas

Great Skua

Pomarine Skua

Arctic Skua

light phase

dark phase

Long-tailed Skua

Gulls

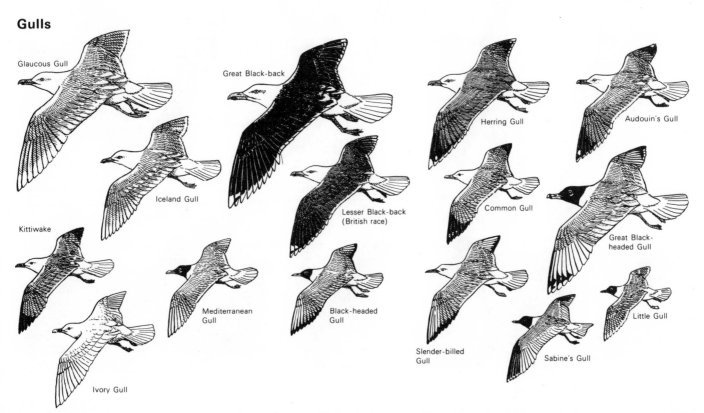

Glaucous Gull

Great Black-back

Herring Gull

Audouin's Gull

Iceland Gull

Common Gull

Kittiwake

Lesser Black-back
(British race)

Great Black-
headed Gull

Mediterranean
Gull

Black-headed
Gull

Little Gull

Slender-billed
Gull

Sabine's Gull

Ivory Gull

Terns

Black Tern

White-winged Black Tern

Gull-billed Tern

Whiskered Tern

Sandwich Tern

Common Tern

Little Tern

Arctic Tern

Caspian Tern

Roseate Tern

Auks

Razorbill

Guillemot (bridled form)

Brünnich's Guillemot

Black Guillemot

Little Auk

Puffin

Artist: Manfred Pforr

Special Section
The Breeding Birds of Europe

Black-throated Diver (Gavia arctica)

Black-throated Divers nest on large, deep inland waters, sometimes in forested areas. The nest is usually a small heap of moss or other vegetation close to the water's edge on a small island. Occasionally the nest may be on the shore of the lake, and where material is plentiful a larger nest may be built using twigs and other vegetation. Food, which consists mainly of fish with small crabs, snails and vegetable matter, is obtained by diving. The species rarely visits salt water during the breeding season, though birds nesting near the coast may obtain food there if there is a shortage at the nesting locality.

They are solitary nesters, shunning the company of other divers, though several pairs may breed on a large lake where there are many islands. The territory is large and vigorously defended against intruders; the ♂ is highly vocal.

The species winters in sheltered coastal waters along the North Sea coasts of Britain and continental Europe, the southern Baltic, the Atlantic coasts of Britain and France, the eastern Mediterranean and the Black Sea. It sometimes winters on large expanses of fresh water. Generally solitary, it rarely forms even loose flocks in winter.

Migration: Autumn movements from September, mostly October and November. In spring from March to mid-June, mainly April and May.

The larger Great Northern Diver breeds in Iceland: it occasionally summers in Britain and has bred here.

Length:	58–68 cm
Length of wing:	31 cm
Weight:	2000–3000 gm (summer)
Call:	A barking 'kowk' and 'kwuk-kwuk-kwuk'; also 'kra-ōō'
Breeding period:	End of April, May–June first brood of the year. A replacement clutch is possible
Size of clutch:	2 (1–3) eggs
Colour of egg:	Olive brown to dark brown, with a few blackish spots
Size of egg:	84 × 52 mm
Incubation:	28–30 days, broods from first egg onward
Fledging period:	Nidifugous; accompanied by parents at least until able to fly at two months, then independent

bove and left) Ad., Sweden, June 1977 (Ar)

Ad. turning its eggs, Sweden, June 1977 (Ar)

Sweden, 1.7.1968 (Ar)

Red-throated Diver (Gavia stellata)

Red-throated Divers breed on inland waters, often on tiny, shallow pools, though deeper lakes and marine inlets may be used. Like other divers, the nest is situated close to the water's edge; sometimes only a scrape is made, though moss and other vegetation may be used at times. The nest site may be hidden in grass or other waterside plants. On larger lakes food may be obtained in fresh water, but birds breeding in coastal sites may obtain food exclusively in marine waters. The food is almost entirely fish, though some invertebrates, molluscs and crustaceans are also taken. They are generally solitary nesters, though loose colonies are recorded in certain areas. The birds are extremely vocal during the breeding season and spend more time on the wing than other divers, overflying the breeding sites uttering the flight-cackle call.

The species winters in sheltered coastal waters from parts of Iceland and Norway in the north, round the coasts of Britain and Ireland, the Channel and Atlantic coasts of France and Spain. Smaller numbers winter in the Mediterranean and on large inland waters. Eastern birds winter on the Black and Caspian Seas. Some birds may remain on coastal waters close to the breeding area. In winter loose flocks may be formed and small flocks may occur on migration.

Migration: Some birds leave the breeding areas from late August, though their main passage is in October and early November. Birds return to nesting areas from March with the main passage in April.

Length:	53–58 cm
Length of wing:	28 cm
Weight:	1400–1900 gm
Call:	In flight, a cackle like that of the Black-throated Diver, but higher; otherwise 'Miaoo' and 'Owowaa' or 'Ockockerr'
Breeding period:	Mid-May–June. Replacement clutch possible
Size of clutch:	2 (1–3) eggs
Colour of egg:	Olive brown to dark brown, with a few black flecks
Size of egg:	75 × 48 mm
Incubation:	26–28 days, broods from first egg onward
Fledging period:	Nidifugous; under parental care at least until able to fly at six weeks

Winter plumage, Amrum, West Germany, Nov. 1972 (Qu)

Foula, June 1974 (Zi)

ula, June 1973 (Zi)

t) Ad. feeding young, Foula, Shetland, July 1974 (Zi)

29

Great Crested Grebe (Podiceps cristatus)

During the breeding season Great Crested Grebes frequent shallow inland waters ranging from large lakes to small ponds and slow-flowing rivers. Food, which is mainly fish, is obtained by diving; some aquatic invertebrates and plant matter are also taken.

The nest is a large structure of aquatic vegetation with a shallow cup to contain the eggs. It is concealed in reeds or other plants and may be free-floating, tethered or built up from the bottom. Nests are usually solitary, though colonies are found where conditions are favourable.

The species has a striking courtship ritual with ceremonial dances which lead to mating. Hostility is shown to sexual and territorial rivals, though in colonial sites the territory is reduced to the immediate environs of the nest.

Great Crested Grebes are mostly migratory, though some individuals may be resident. Short moult-migrations are undertaken, and many birds move to marine waters in winter, though in central Europe large concentrations are found on inland waters. Birds are forced to move from northern and eastern breeding areas due to lakes freezing in winter, flying to the Mediterranean coast, including North Africa.

Migration: Birds disperse from late July with main movements in late September to early November. Return passage in spring from late February to early May.

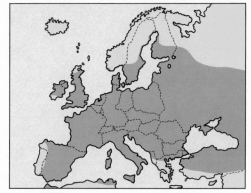

Length:	48 cm
Length of wing:	♂ 19 cm, ♀ 18 cm
Weight:	♂ 1100 g, ♀ 900 g
Call:	'Kruck kruck' or 'Kuck kuck'; also a creaking 'arrr'
Breeding period:	Mid-April to July, 1 or 2 broods a year. Replacement clutch common
Size of clutch:	4 (2–6) eggs
Colour of eggs:	Fresh white with bluish sheen; as breeding progresses brownish, spotted with nesting material
Size of egg:	53 × 36 mm
Incubation:	27–29 days
Fledging period:	Precocial and semi-nidifugous; parental care for 3–4 weeks

...ung bird in the wing-pockets of an adult, Bavaria, ...ne 1969 (Pf)

...ft) Pair of great crested grebes in breeding habitat, Bavaria, West Germany, June 1969 (Pf)

Ad. making its nest, Bavaria, 6.8.73 (Pf)

Newly hatched young in nest, Bavaria, 6.6.1972 (Pf)

31

Red-necked Grebe

(Podiceps griseigena)

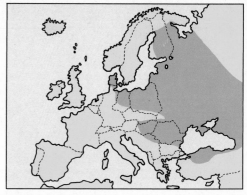

Red-necked Grebes breed on shallow, inland waters with large amounts of emergent vegetation. Food, which is chiefly invertebrates, is obtained by diving or swimming on the surface with the head submerged. In winter fish may predominate in the diet. Like the Great Crested Grebe, they have complex rituals of courtship and display. They are the least gregarious of the grebes.

The nest is a floating heap of aquatic vegetation, anchored to submerged vegetation. It is usually sited in emergent vegetation. Nests are normally solitary, though loose colonies may be formed. Nests are often found in association with other waterbirds such as Black-headed Gull colonies. The species is migratory, wintering in coastal waters on the Atlantic coast of Norway, the southern Baltic, North Sea coasts of England, Denmark and the Low Countries. Some birds winter in the Adriatic and Agean Seas, and some are found on the larger lakes of central Europe.

Migration: Birds disperse from the breeding areas from late July with the main movements in September to early November. In spring, return passage occurs from late February, mostly late March to April.

Length:	43 cm
Length of wing:	17 cm
Weight:	820 g
Call:	In courtship 'Gagagag' or 'keck-keck'; also a whinnying 'uuuuoh'
Breeding period:	Mid-April, May, June, 1 or 2 broods per year. Replacement clutch common
Size of clutch:	4–5 (2–6) eggs
Colour of egg:	White, generally with brown spots from nest material like the eggs of all diving birds
Size of egg:	50 × 33 mm
Incubation:	20–23 days
Fledging period:	Precocial and semi-nidifugous; parental care for at least 10 weeks

nsitional plumage, Starnberger See (Bavaria), cember 1976 (Kü)
ft) Einfelder See, Holstein, West Germany, June 1967 (Qu)

Ad. with young in its back feathers, Schleswig-Holstein, West Germany (Ar)

Schleswig-Holstein, May 1969 (Pf)

Black-necked Grebe (Podiceps nigricollis)

Black-necked Grebes breed on small, shallow inland waters with considerable emergent vegetation and a rich supply of food. Less dependent on fish than other grebes, the main diet is insects and larvae with some crustaceans and small fish. Food is obtained by surface-skimming and by swimming with the head submerged. Some insects are taken from just above the surface. The most gregarious of the grebes, they have a typically complex ritual of courtship behaviour.

The nest is a heap of aquatic vegetation anchored to aquatic plants. The species is usually colonial with nests quite close together, often in association with colonies of *Larus* gulls or other waterbirds. There is great irregularity in the choice of breeding sites. This is in part due to the drying up of shallow lakes or exhaustion of food supply. Large colonies may flourish for many years then completely disappear to be re-formed elsewhere.

Except on some central European lakes the species is migratory, wintering in coastal waters or large inland lakes. Most winter on the coasts of Britain, France and Iberia, with others south to North Africa, and eastwards in the Adriatic, Agean and Black Seas.

Migration: Dispersal from mid-August with main passage in late September to November. Spring passage from mid-March to May, mostly April.

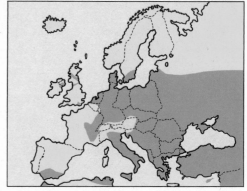

Length:	30 cm
Length of wing:	13 cm
Weight:	300 g
Call:	Trill like that of a little grebe; also 'pee-eep' and 'bidder-vidder'
Breeding period:	End of May, June, 1 brood per year. Replacement clutch common
Size of clutch:	3–4 (2–6) eggs
Colour of egg:	White, with brown discoloration after longer breeding
Size of egg:	44 × 30 mm
Incubation:	20–22 days
Fledging period:	Precocious and semi-nidifugous; parental care for 3–4 weeks

d of nesting, ♀ on nest, Seewinkel, 1965 (Li)

'(t) Nesting Black-headed Grebe, Seewinkel, Austria, 1965 (Li)

Winter plumage, Starnberger See, Bavaria, January 1975 (Kü)

Nest with eggs in rising water, Neusiedler See, Austria, 1962 (Li)

Little Grebe (Tachybaptus ruficollis)

The Little Grebe is the smallest of the European breeding grebes and has the widest choice of nesting habitat, ranging from small pools and slow rivers to large lakes. It generally favours shallow water with some emergent vegetation. Food consists of insects, larvae, crustaceans, small fish and molluscs. It is obtained chiefly by diving, though insects are taken from just above the surface, and the species will leap out of the water in pursuit of prey.

Little Grebes take to the wing more readily than other grebes and are also particularly vocal. This is especially true during courtship ceremonies.

The nest is the usual floating platform of aquatic vegetation, anchored to submerged vegetation or to overhanging twigs. The nest is solitary and the territory is defended rigorously.

Little Grebes are less migratory than other grebes. Many are resident whilst others merely disperse to larger expanses of water. It is rarely found on the open sea, though harbours and sheltered inlets are used, particularly in severe weather. Birds from northern and eastern Europe move west or south-west in winter.

Migration: Dispersal from late July with main movements in September–October. Returning from late February, mostly March and April.

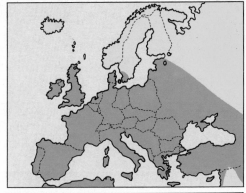

Length:	27 cm
Length of wing:	10 cm
Weight:	150–200 g
Call:	Typical trill, something like 'bibibibibi' or 'priiii'
Breeding period:	Mid-April, May, June, July, 2–3 broods per year. Replacement clutch frequent
Size of clutch:	4–6 eggs
Colour of egg:	White, generally with irregular brown markings
Size of egg:	38 × 26 mm
Incubation:	20–21 days
Fledging period:	Precocial and semi-nidifugous; parental care for 30–40 days, able to fly at 44–48 days

nter plumage, Bavaria, Amper, 1958 (Li)

Chick, Bavaria, May 1975 (Pa)

Fresh clutch, Bavaria, Amper-Altwasser, 1960 (Li)

ft) Ad. nesting, Bavaria, Amper-Altwasser, West Germany, 1960 (Li)

Fulmar (Fulmarus glacialis)

The Fulmar is one of the commonest seabirds of northern waters, having undergone a remarkable expansion of range in the last 200 years. It breeds on cliff-ledges, old buildings, slopes and banks and among sand-dunes. Most sites are close to the sea but inland sites are known.

Food is obtained entirely at sea and consists of crustaceans, fish and fish-offal and carrion. The species is highly gregarious, breeding in large colonies: feeding flocks of several thousand may occur where food is abundant.

Fulmars attend breeding colonies for most of the year, spending only a month or two at sea after breeding. The egg is laid on bare rock or earth with no nesting materials; both sexes share incubation and the care of the chick. Fulmars are masters of flying, spending long periods wheeling effortlessly around the breeding sites. They are noisy and often aggressive towards each other. Both adults and young have the ability to eject stomach-oil in territorial or feeding disputes.

Adult birds are largely resident, though there is some pelagic dispersal. Young birds, which take at least six years to reach maturity, make longer pelagic movements.

Migration: Autumn dispersal after breeding in September and October.

Length:	47 cm
Length of wing:	31 cm
Weight:	800 g
Call:	In colonies, and feeding flocks, grunting, squeaking, groaning and cackling noises
Breeding period:	Mid-May, June, 1 brood per year. No replacement clutch
Size of clutch:	1 (2) eggs
Colour of eggs:	White
Size of eggs:	74 × 51 mm
Incubation:	52–53 days
Fledging period:	Nidicolous; remain at nest under parental care until able to fly at 46–57 days

la, April 1974 (Zi)

t) Foula, Shetland, April 1974 (Zi)

Ad. with chick, Foula, July 1974 (Zi)

Rundø, Norway, 27.6.1966 (Sy)

39

Gannet (Sula bassana)

The Gannet is the largest seabird breeding in Europe. It nests in dense colonies on selected islands or mainland cliffs. Food, which is almost entirely fish, is obtained by spectacular plunge-diving or by swimming with head submerged and then diving from the surface.

Gannets build a nest from seaweed, grass, feathers and scraps of fishing net or rope. The nest is used in successive years and may become quite large. In dense colonies nests are very close together, even touching. Gannets have a marked sense of territory and defend their nest-space vigorously.

Both sexes share in nest-building, incubation and care of the chick. At the breeding colonies the birds are noisy and have a complex display. Established breeding colonies tend to expand, and there is a reluctance to form new colonies; the entire eastern Atlantic population breeds in only thirty colonies.

Young birds leave the nest before they are able to fly and disperse by swimming. Most birds are at least partly migratory, some moving south to the coasts of North Africa, others entering the Mediterranean.

Migration: dispersal from August, mostly September–October, birds returning to breeding colonies in January to March.

Length:	92 cm
Length of wing:	49 cm
Weight:	3000 g
Call:	Hoarse crackling sounds, 'urrah', mainly at the nesting places
Breeding period:	Beginning of April, May, 1 brood per year. Replacement clutch frequent
Size of clutch:	1 (2) eggs
Colour of eggs:	Blue-green shell, often unrecognisable because of the white coating of chalk
Size of eggs:	79 × 50 mm
Incubation:	42–46 days
Fledging period:	Nidicolous; cared for by parents till independent at about 90 days

ss Rock, Scotland, June 1976 (Zi)

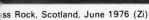

ft) Hermaness, Shetland, July 1974 (Zi)

Bass Rock, June 1976 (Pa)

Ad. on clutch, Bass Rock, June 1976 (Pa)

41

Cormorant (Phalacrocorax carbo)

Cormorants are found on both salt and fresh water. They frequent sheltered seas, estuaries, extensive inland waters, large rivers and other wetland. They breed on cliffs, in trees, reedbeds and occasionally on the ground. Food, which is almost entirely fish, is caught by surface-diving. They are often persecuted by man due to alleged competition for food, though most fish taken are not marketable species.

Cormorants nest in colonies, sometimes up to thousands of pairs. The nest is built of twigs or seaweed and other vegetable matter. Both sexes share in nest-building, incubation and care of the young.

British birds are not migratory, but disperse after breeding. Most other European populations migrate, either westwards to the coasts of France and Iberia or south into the Mediterranean.

Migration: Dispersal from breeding colonies as early as mid-June, but main movements in August to October, returning in February and March.

Length:	92 cm
Length of wing:	35 cm
Weight:	2000–2800 g
Call:	Only at nesting place: 'krokrokro' or 'chrochrochro'; also 'krao' or 'kraorr'
Breeding period:	April, May, June, 1 brood per year. Further laying frequent
Size of clutch:	3–4 (6) eggs
Colour of eggs:	Light blue shell hardly visible through chalky white deposit
Size of eggs:	66 × 41 mm, very variable
Incubation:	28–31 days
Fledging period:	Nidicolous; fledge at about 50 days but parental care for further 40–50 days

nger Stausee, Bavaria, West Germany, Spring 1975
) Pair of Cormorants nesting (Li)

Young demanding food (Li)

Cormorant's nest (Li)

43

Shag (Phalacrocorax aristotelis)

Shags are essentially marine, breeding on rocky coastlines and preferring deeper water than Cormorants. Food, which is almost entirely fish, is caught by surface-diving, though plunge-diving has been recorded.

Shags nest on cliff-ledges, in caves and among boulder beaches. The nest is built of seaweed and other plant materials; the species usually breeds in colonies, though nests are widely spaced. Both sexes share in nest-building, incubation and care of the young. Shags have an elaborate courtship display and are aggressive towards intruders at the nest site. The female is almost voiceless, but the male is loud and noisy.

Shags do not migrate but there is considerable dispersal away from breeding colonies particularly from the northern part of the range. The Mediterranean race is largely resident.

Migration: Dispersal from early July, mostly August–October, returning in February and March. Young birds move further than adults.

Length:	76 cm
Length of wing:	27 cm
Weight:	1750 g
Call:	♀ mostly mute; ♂ at breeding place 'Arrk, arrk' or 'croak, cryke, croak'
Breeding period:	Beginning of April, May, June, 1 brood per year. Replacement clutch frequent
Size of clutch:	3 (2–6) eggs
Colour of eggs:	Blue-green, with irregular white chalky deposits
Size of eggs:	63 × 38 mm
Incubation:	30–31 days
Fledging period:	Nidicolous; they leave the nest after about 50 days and are under parental care for a further 20–50 days

on nest, Rundø, July 1976 (Di)

) Rundø, Norway, July 1976 (Di)

Young bird, Rundø, July 1976 (Di)

Rundø, July 1976 (Di)

White Pelican (Pelecanus onocrotalus)

White Pelicans frequent areas of warm, shallow fresh water, river deltas and, to a lesser extent, brackish or saline waters. They are exclusively fish-eaters, obtaining their food by scooping with the huge bill, holding the fish in the gular pouch. They sometimes indulge in co-operative fishing, with groups forming a semi-circle.

The European population has suffered a marked decline due to human persecution and drainage of marshes.

They are gregarious birds, nesting in colonies of a few hundred to several thousand pairs. The nests are built in thick vegetation, on islands or reedbeds, sometimes on open ground. The nest is a large structure of reeds, twigs and other vegetable matter, built by the ♀ with materials brought by the ♂. Both sexes share incubation and care of the young. After 2—3 weeks the young form crèches.

White Pelicans are peaceful birds, showing little antagonism towards others.

European and Turkish birds are migratory, moving to Egypt, the Red Sea coast and perhaps further south in Africa.

Migration: Disperse from breeding colonies from early September with main movements in late September and October, returning from early March, mostly April.

Length:	150–180 cm
Length of wing:	62 '–68 cm
Weight:	10.5 kg
Call:	Booming, rattling calls at the breeding place, otherwise grunting noises
Breeding period:	Mid-April, May, June, 1 brood per year. Replacement clutch possible
Size of clutch:	2 (1–3) eggs
Colour of eggs:	White, with yellowish chalky deposit
Size of eggs:	94 × 59 mm, very variable
Incubation:	30 days
Fledging period:	Nidicolous; but leaves the nest after about 20 days to form groups of young. Independent at 2½ months

tolia, 1975 (Li)

) Central Anatolia, Turkey, 24.5.1970 (Sy)

Young birds of different ages, Anatolia, 1971 (Wa)

Anatolia, 1971 (Wa)

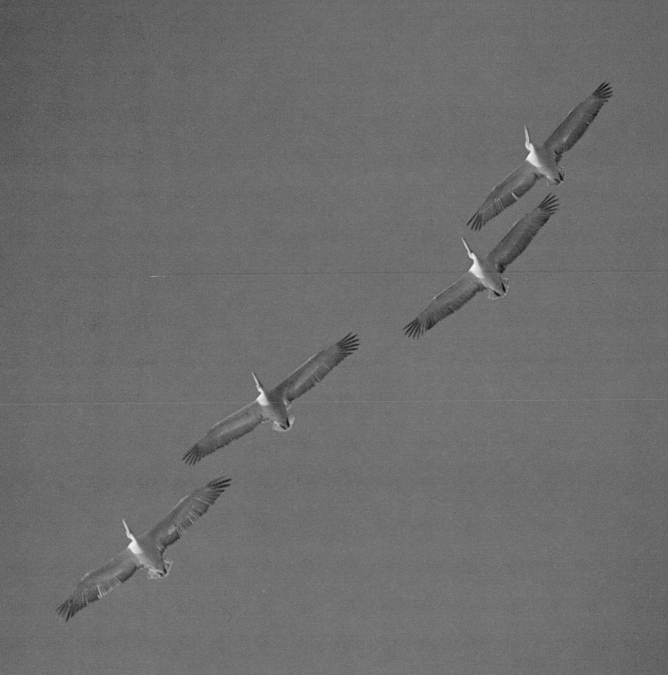

Dalmatian Pelican

(Pelecanus crispus)

The Dalmatian Pelican frequents habitat similar to that of the White Pelican, but it inhabits more mountainous areas and tends to be less coastal.

It is colonial, with nests often touching, though loose colonies are known. It often breeds alongside White Pelicans though in discrete groups. The nests are generally more substantial than those of the White Pelican, being a large heap of grass, twigs and reeds cemented with droppings. Materials are brought in by the ♂ and the ♀ builds the nest. Both sexes share in incubation, though the ♀ takes the larger share.

Food is entirely fish, caught by scooping, often group-fishing.

The population in Europe has suffered a decline due to human persecution and loss of habitat.

The migration is not well studied but birds probably winter away from the breeding areas in the east Mediterranean, Turkey and Egypt.

Migration: Dispersal from breeding colonies from August, mostly September, returning in late February or March.

Length:	160–180 cm
Length of wing:	70 cm
Weight:	10.5 kg
Call:	In the colonies grunting, barking, hissing, spitting and rattling noises can be heard
Breeding period:	Beginning of April, May, June (July), 1 brood per year
Size of clutch:	2–3 (5–6) eggs
Colour of eggs:	White, stained with brown
Size of eggs:	95 × 60 mm, but very variable
Incubation:	30–32 days
Fledging period:	Nidicolous; young birds of a colony form crèche groups at 2½ weeks. Independent at 3½ months

rthern Greece, 30.4.1972 (Si)

Central Anatolia, 10.5.1971 (Sy)

Central Anatolia, 11.5.1971 (Sy)

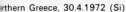
t) Central Anatolia, Turkey, 1974 (Li)

49

Grey Heron (Ardea cinerea)

Grey Herons favour low-lying areas with shallow fresh water including rivers, lakes, pools and marshes. They can also be found on estuaries, mudflats and sandy shores. They take a wide variety of food including fish, amphibians, small mammals and reptiles. Food is obtained along water-margins where the Heron wades or stands motionless, grabbing or stabbing suitable prey.

Herons are colonial nesters, though single nests are known. The nest is built of twigs and is usually sited in a tree or bush. In some areas Herons nest in reedbeds using reeds as nesting material: occasionally they nest on cliffs. The ♂ brings most of the nesting material while the ♀ builds. Both sexes share in incubation and care of the young.

The British population is non-migratory, but birds disperse over a wide area. From other European populations birds migrate mainly south-west into France and Iberia, some to North Africa and even into tropical Africa. Birds from eastern populations move to the Agean, Turkey and Egypt.

Migration: British birds disperse from mid-June, most moving in September—October, returning in February and March.

Length:	90 cm
Length of wing:	46 cm
Weight:	1600 g
Call:	In flight, typically 'Frarnk', on the nest 'ro, ro'; also grunting, gurgling and scratching noises. Young beg by squealing
Breeding period:	March, April, May, 1, rarely 2, broods per year. Replacement clutch regular
Size of clutch:	3–5 (2–7) eggs
Colour of eggs:	Pale blue-green
Size of eggs:	61 × 43 mm
Incubation:	25–26 days
Fledging period:	Nidicolous; they start to fly at about 50 days, returning to the nest for a further 10–20 days before becoming independent

of Grey Herons courting, Baden-Württemberg,
st Germany, 10.4.1967 (Pf)
) Ad. preening, Bavaria, West Germany (Li)

Bavaria, 8.8.1975 (Pf)

Marchauen, Lower Austria, 28.3.1976 (Nek)

Purple Heron (Ardea purpurea)

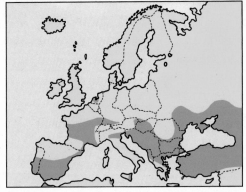

The Purple Heron is found in areas of dense marshland vegetation such as reedbeds. It feeds chiefly on fish and insects, but will also take amphibians and small mammals. It sometimes feeds by wading or, more often, by standing motionless against a background of dense vegetation. It nests in dense reedbeds, usually near open water. The nest is built of dead reedstems and is sited on a clump of dead reeds: sometimes tree-nests are built. The species breeds in loose colonies, often of only two to five pairs, sometimes in association with other herons, including Grey Heron.

Both sexes share in nest-building, incubation and care of young. Purple Herons are a summer-visitor to Europe. Though a few may overwinter in the Mediterranean, most migrate south of the Sahara to winter in tropical Africa. When returning to their breeding areas in spring a few birds overshoot under favourable conditions and reach Britain and Northern Europe.

Migration: Dispersal from breeding colonies from mid-July, main autumn passage in late August–October. Spring passage mostly March and April.

Length:	80 cm
Length of wing:	37 cm
Weight:	600–1100 g
Call:	In flight 'krreck'; on nest, resembles those of Grey Heron
Breeding period:	End of April, May, June (July), 1 brood per year. Replacement clutch regular
Size of clutch:	4–5 (up to 8) eggs
Colour of eggs:	Vivid blue-green
Size of eggs:	57 × 41 mm
Incubation:	26 days
Fledging period:	Nidicolous; leaves nest and clambers into reeds from 8–10 days, fledging at 45–50 days and independent at 55–65 days

. approaching nest, north-east Greece, 29.5.1969 (Sy)   Young birds, Hessen, West Germany, 17.7.1968 (Sy)   Greece, 1973 (Li)

ft) Purple Heron on guard, Seewinkel, Austria, 1965 (Li)

53

Little Egret (Egretta garzetta)

The Little Egret is found in rather open areas with shallow lakes, lagoons and ricefields. It also frequents estuaries and coastal waters. It feeds mainly on small fish, amphibians, both terrestrial and aquatic insects, reptiles, worms and molluscs. Food is obtained both by stalking and by running and snapping at prey in shallow water.

It is a colonial nester, breeding in large heronries, often in company with other species. The nest is a platform of sticks or reeds, usually in trees, though sometimes in reedbeds or bushes. The nest is built mainly by the ♀ using materials brought in by the ♂. Both sexes share incubation and care of the young.

The Little Egret is migratory; a few winter in the Mediterranean and North Africa, but most migrate over the Sahara to winter in tropical Africa. The young disperse at random after fledging, depending on abundance of food, then gradually move south.

Migration: Dispersal from mid-July with main movements from late August to November, returning in March and April, when some may overshoot to Britain and northern Europe.

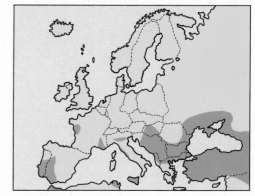

Length:	58 cm
Wing length:	27 cm
Weight:	500 g
Call:	Grating, scratching cries, only heard at breeding place
Breeding period:	End of April, May, June (July), 1 brood per year. Replacement clutch possible
Size of clutch:	3–5 (–8) eggs
Colour of eggs:	Light blue-green
Size of eggs:	46 × 34 mm
Incubation:	21–22 days
Fledging period:	Nidicolous; at 30 days they clamber about around the nest. Able to fly at 6 weeks, independent at 7–8 weeks

hern Greece, 1977 (Li)

Young birds, Camargue, France, 1967 (Li)

Manyas-Gölü, Turkey, 2.6.1966 (Fe)

Northern Greece, 28.8.1975 (Pf)

Great White Egret (Egretta alba)

The Great White Egret is a bird of extensive marsh and wetlands of eastern Europe. During the wet season it feeds mainly on fish and aquatic insects, changing to a diet of small mammals and terrestrial insects under dry conditions.

It nests colonially, often in association with Grey or Purple Herons in extensive reedbeds. The nest is a large structure of reeds or twigs, usually sited in dense reeds, but sometimes in low trees. Both sexes take part in nest-building, incubation and care of the young.

The species suffered from human persecution at the turn of the century when the decorative breeding plumes were in demand by the millinery trade. Now it is threatened by drainage and loss of habitat.

Great White Egrets are less migratory than other European egrets. They disperse from the breeding colonies, moving south to winter on the Adriatic and eastern Mediterranean. Smaller numbers winter in Tunisia and a few in southern France.

Migration: Dispersal from mid-June with main movements away from breeding areas in September–October. In spring, return passage from mid-February to late April, mostly March.

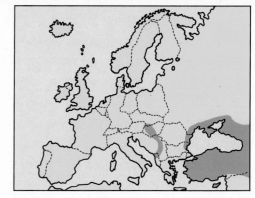

Length:	89 cm
Wing length:	43 cm
Weight:	1500 g
Call:	'Rroo, rroo', only at breeding place; also croaking calls
Breeding period:	Mid-April, May, June, 1 brood per year
Size of clutch:	3–4 (2–6) eggs
Colour of eggs:	Light blue
Size of eggs:	61 × 43 mm
Incubation:	25–26 days
Fledging period:	Nidicolous; leaves nest at about 20 days and wanders to other nests. Fledge at 42 days remaining with parents till dispersal

...winkel, 1965 (Li)

Ad. seeking food, Seewinkel, Austria, 1965 (Li)

Seewinkel, 1962 (Li)

Juvenile, Seewinkel, 1962 (Li)

57

Squacco Heron (Ardeola ralloides)

The Squacco Heron frequents areas of bushy swampland, overgrown rivers and ditches and small ponds. It will also feed in more open areas including flooded fields. It feeds chiefly on small fish, insects and amphibians and is mostly crepuscular, though will feed in daytime.

It nests in dense thickets, reedbeds and in trees, usually in scattered groups or in mixed colonies of other herons. The nest is built of twigs or reeds depending on site and is built mainly by the ♀ with materials brought by the ♂. Incubation is mostly by the ♀, though both parents feed the young. Though the species suffered a decline in numbers due to the plume-trade and to loss of habitat there are now signs that it is increasing in many areas.

The species is a summer visitor to Europe, though a few individuals may winter in North Africa and the Mediterranean. The majority make a trans-Saharan crossing to winter in tropical Africa.

Migration: Main autumn movements in late August to early November, returning in March and April.

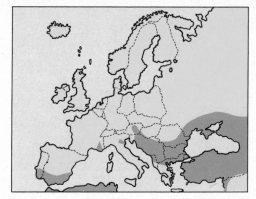

Length:	46 cm
Wing length:	21 cm
Weight:	290 g
Call:	A hoarse 'karr', only in the breeding season
Breeding period:	Mid-May, June, July, 1 brood per year
Size of clutch:	4–6 eggs
Colour of eggs:	Pale blue-green
Size of eggs:	39 × 28 mm
Incubation:	22–24 days
Fledging period:	Nidicolous; the young leave the nest at about 30 days and clamber about in the colony till fledging at 45 days

ing for food, Camargue, 1967 (Li)

Camargue, France, 1967 (Li)

Manyas-Gölü, Turkey, 4.6.1970 (Sy)

Manyas-Gölü, 4.6.1970 (Sy)

59

Night Heron (Nycticorax nycticorax)

Night Herons are found in bushy areas of marshland or uncleared pastureland. The species is markedly crepuscular, roosting by day in thick cover. Food is mainly amphibians, fish and insects, and is obtained by stalking in shallow water or by standing motionless at water margins. During the breeding season it will feed during the day to bring back food for the young. It is a colonial nester, often in association with other Herons, Glossy Ibis or Pygmy Cormorants. The nest is a platform of twigs and sticks, usually sited in trees or low bushes, though reedbeds are used on occasion. The ♀ builds the nest with materials brought by the ♂; the ♀ takes the major share of incubation and both sexes share in rearing the young.

The Night Heron is migratory, only a few birds remaining in Europe over the winter. Most make a trans-Saharan crossing to winter in tropical Africa, though some winter in Egypt and the southern Caspian.

Migration: Dispersal from breeding colonies from mid-July with main movements in September—November. Most spring migrants return in March and April.

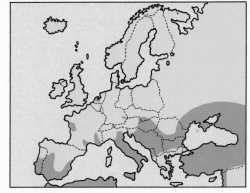

Length:	61 cm
Wing length:	29 cm
Weight:	600 g
Call:	In flight: 'Whack' or 'Quark'. At breeding place: hoarse croaking and squealing in many variants
Breeding period:	End of April, May, June, 1, sometimes 2, broods. Replacement clutch frequent
Size of clutch:	3–5 (1–8) eggs
Colour of eggs:	Blue-green, pale
Size of eggs:	50 × 36 mm
Incubation:	21–22 days
Fledging period:	Nidicolous; after 3 weeks they climb around about the nest. Able to fly at 40–50 days, independent soon after

nyas-Gölü, 15.6.1966 (Fe)

Juvenile, Camargue, France, 1967 (Li)

Manyas-Gölü, 30.6.1970 (Sy)

) Manyas-Gölü, Turkey, May 1971 (Zi)

Little Bittern (Ixobrychus minutus)

The Little Bittern is the smallest European representative of the Heron family. It is found in low-lying areas of marsh, margins of rivers and lakes where there is a dense growth of reeds or other vegetation. The species is crepuscular, feeding on fish, amphibians and insects which it catches by standing quietly at the water's edge, often in cover of reeds.

The species will climb about on reedstems and, when alarmed, will 'freeze' in a vertical posture with the bill pointing skywards.

The nest site is usually in reeds, though sometimes in low bushes. Nests are usually solitary, though several pairs may nest in close proximity. Both sexes share incubation, the ♀ at night and the ♂ by day.

The species is a summer visitor to Europe, wintering in tropical Africa. Migration usually takes place at night, though large numbers have been seen in migration in daylight on the Egyptian coast.

Migration: Autumn passage from August to November, with return passage in March–May, mostly April.

Length:	36 cm
Wing length:	15 cm
Weight:	148 g
Call:	♂ Courting: 'Vrugh' repeated at 2-second intervals. In flight: hoarse 'quer'
Breeding period:	Mid-May, June, July, 1, sometimes 2 broods per year. Replacement clutch regular
Size of clutch:	5–6 (4–9) eggs
Colour of eggs:	White
Size of eggs:	36 × 26 mm
Incubation:	17–19 days
Fledging period:	Nidicolous; young leave the nest at 17–18 days. Able to fly at about 1 month

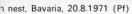

n nest, Bavaria, 20.8.1971 (Pf)

) ♂ on nest, Bavaria, West Germany, 20.8.1971 (Pf)

Ad. ♂ in reed-clump, Bavaria, 2.6.1958 (Pf)

Late clutch with young, Bavaria, 14.8.1971 (Pf)

Bittern (Botaurus stellaris)

The Bittern is found in lowland swamps and wetland, where there is plenty of dense cover, particularly reedbeds. It is a solitary, skulking bird, essentially crepuscular in habits. It feeds chiefly on fish, amphibians and insects, though small mammals and birds are also taken. Both adults and young will adopt a vertical stance with the bill pointing upwards when alarmed.

The nest is a loose heap of reeds and other vegetation. Some birds are polygamous and several females may nest close together. Usually the female builds the nest and incubates the eggs, though the male may help in monogamous pairs. The female is largely responsible for rearing the young, though the ♂♂ will bring food to the nest.

Despite their large size, Bitterns are quite agile and will clamber about in reeds clutching bunches of stems.

Bitterns are partially migratory, moving away from breeding areas in freezing conditions. Most winter in the milder parts of western Europe, though some may migrate to Africa.

Migration: Dispersal from breeding areas from late July, mostly September–November. Hard-weather movements take place in winter, birds returning to breeding areas in February–April, mostly March.

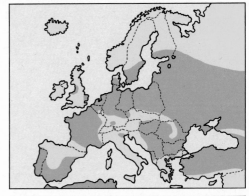

Length:	76 cm
Wing length:	31–34 cm
Weight:	1100 g
Call:	♂ While courting, mostly at night, a deep and far-carrying 'ehumb'. In flight, 'kau'
Breeding period:	Mid-April, May (June), 1 brood per year. Replacement clutch frequent
Size of clutch:	5–6 (3–7) eggs
Colour of eggs:	Olive-brown
Size of eggs:	53 × 38 mm
Incubation:	25–26 days
Fledging period:	Nidicolous; at 2 weeks they climb out of the nest for short distances, able to fly at 50–55 days and independent soon after

on guard, Bavaria, 13.4.1971 (Li)

◄) Ad. hunting, summer in Bavaria, West Germany, 1970 (Li)

♀ incubating, Rantum-Becken, Sylt, June 1968 (Qu)

Upper Lusatia (Mak)

White Stork (Ciconia ciconia)

White Storks frequent open farmland, meadows and wetlands with scattered trees. They take a wide range of live food including reptiles and amphibians, insects, small mammals and crustaceans. Where food is abundant flocks may feed together.

White Storks nest in tall trees, on high buildings and on specially erected platforms. The nest is a large structure of branches, twigs and other vegetation built by both sexes. The nests are often solitary, but colonies occur in some areas. Both sexes share in incubation and care of the young. The adults have a complicated display, with much bill-clattering and ritual posturing.

The White Stork is a popular bird and is protected by man over much of its range. However, there has been a decrease in the population over much of Europe, possibly due to habitat destruction and pesticide poisoning, though the reasons for this decline are not fully understood.

The species is highly migratory, huge flocks migrating through the Bosphorus and Gibraltar to avoid a long Mediterranean crossing. They winter in Africa, as far south as Cape Province. Small numbers winter in the southern parts of Iberia and in the Middle East.

Migration: From mid-August to November, returning from February to May, mostly March and early April.

Length:	102 cm
Wing length:	57 cm
Weight:	3500 g
Call:	Adults almost mute apart from clattering their beaks; the young hiss, mew and cheep
Breeding period:	April, May, 1 brood per year. Replacement clutch possible
Size of clutch:	4 (1–7) eggs
Colour of eggs:	White
Size of eggs:	73 × 52 mm, variable
Incubation:	33–34 days
Fledging period:	Nidicolous; leave nest at 58–64 days. Independent at 70 days

hunting, Anatolia, Turkey, 1974 (Li)

Seewinkel, Austria, 1962 (Li)

Young birds, Anatolia, 1977 (Li)

) Nest in tree, Macedonia, Yugoslavia, 1972 (Li)

67

Black Stork (Ciconia nigra)

Black Storks are found in large forest areas interspersed with patches of wetland or meadows. Unlike the White Stork, they avoid human habitation and require undisturbed areas. Food is obtained mainly in shallow waters and consists of fish, amphibians, insects and small mammals.

The nest is sited in a large tree or on a cliff-face, and is a large structure of branches, sticks and other vegetation. Both sexes take part in nest-building, incubation and care of young. The species declined in range and numbers, especially in the western part of its range. Though there are signs of an increase in the east it is still a scarce bird in Europe. Some of the Iberian population are resident, but the birds from eastern Europe migrate to winter in Africa. Like White Storks, they prefer short sea-crossings, using the Bosphorus, though some make longer crossings to Tunisia.

Migration: Main autumn movements from mid-September to mid-November, returning in February to May, mostly late March and April.

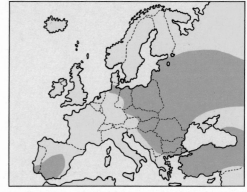

Length:	97 cm
Wing length:	54 cm
Weight:	3000 g
Call:	Little bill-clacking, but an extensive range of calls including 'hhiio' and 'chi-chu'
Breeding period:	End of April, May, 1 brood per year
Size of clutch:	3–5 (2–6) eggs
Colour of eggs:	White
Size of eggs:	65 × 49 mm
Incubation:	32–38 days
Fledging period:	Nidicolous; leave nest at 63–70 days, independent soon after

...nging places for incubation, Black Sea coast, 5.1973 (Li)

...) Ad. on nest, Black Sea coast, Turkey, 25.5.1973 (Li)

Anatolia, Turkey, 1973 (Li)

Black Sea coast, 26.5.1973 (Li)

Spoonbill (Platalea leucorodia)

Because of their specialised feeding requirements Spoonbills are limited to areas of shallow water with sandy or muddy bottoms. The food, which consists mainly of small fish, insects, crustaceans and molluscs, is obtained by a sweeping motion with the bill slightly open whilst wading in shallow water. Spoonbills are gregarious, often feeding in small flocks and nesting colonially. The nests are sited on the ground in reedbeds or in low bushes and trees. The nest is a large pile of reeds, twigs or leaves and other plant material. Both sexes share nest-building, incubation and care of the young.

Spoonbills are migratory, mostly wintering on the coasts of West Africa, though some winter in southern Spain, North Africa, Turkey and the Middle East.

Migration: Dispersal from breeding colonies from mid-July with main movements in late August—October. Return passage from February, mostly March and early April.

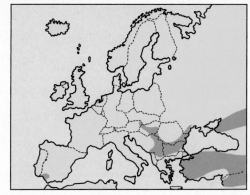

Length:	86 cm
Wing length:	37–39 cm
Weight:	2000 g
Call:	Predominantly silent. At nest, deep grunting and groaning calls
Breeding period:	End of April, May, June (July), 1 brood per year. Replacement clutch possible
Size of clutch:	3–4 (–7) eggs
Colour of eggs:	White, with pale- or reddish-brown specks
Size of eggs:	67 × 47 mm
Incubation:	21–25 days
Fledging period:	Nidicolous; able to leave nest at 4 weeks; fledge at 45–50 days

seeking food, Seewinkel, 1962 (Li)

Seewinkel, Austria, 1962 (Li)

Manyas-Gölü, Turkey, 8.6.1968 (Fe)

Manyas-Gölü, 18.6.1966 (Fe)

71

Glossy Ibis (Plegadis falcinellus)

The Glossy Ibis favours lowland areas of eastern Europe with shallow lakes, lagoons, river deltas and estuaries. They feed mostly in small flocks, wading in shallow water to obtain insects, crustaceans and other small aquatic creatures.

During the breeding season the species frequents marshes and reedbeds. They nest colonially, often in association with other Ciconiiformes or Pygmy Cormorants. The nest is sited in trees or in dense reeds and constructed of twigs or reeds depending on site. Both sexes take part in nest-building, incubation and rearing young, though the ♀ takes the larger share.

There has been a marked decline in numbers in western Europe and the species is now confined to certain localities in eastern Europe.

Glossy Ibis are migratory and prone to wandering: small flocks may occur well outside their breeding areas. Small numbers winter on the Mediterranean coasts and in the Middle East, but most migrate to tropical Africa for the winter.

Migration: Wanders away from colonies from early August. Main migratory movements in September and October. Return passage from March to May, mostly April.

Length:	56 cm
Wing length:	28 cm
Weight:	600 g
Call:	Mostly mute. In flight, a crow-like 'raak'. On the nest, grunts and croaks
Breeding period:	Mid-May, June, July, 1 brood per year
Size of clutch:	3–4 (–6) eggs
Colour of eggs:	Dark blue-green
Size of eggs:	52 × 37 mm
Incubation:	21 days
Fledging period:	Nidicolous; they can leave the nest platform from 14 days. Able to fly at 6 weeks

feeding, Manyas-Gölü, 4.6.1970 (Sy)

) Manyas-Gölü, Turkey, 4.6.1970 (Fe)

Young at about 14 days, Turkey, 5.6.1970 (Sy)

Turkey, 3.6.1970 (Sy)

73

Greater Flamingo

(Phoenicopterus ruber)

Flamingos have very specialised requirements for feeding and nesting. They are found on shallow lakes and lagoons with a high saline or alkaline content. They are essentially gregarious birds, feeding in large groups, filtering invertebrates, crustaceans, molluscs and other aquatic organisms from the mud and water.

Breeding is often erratic and takes place at certain favoured localities such as the Camargue in southern France and in Andalucia. The nests are conical mounds of mud or sand and are constructed close together. Both sexes share in nest-construction, incubation and care of the young. The chicks are fed on a glandular secretion called 'crop-milk'.

The European population is partially migratory. Flocks will overwinter at breeding localities but others move to North Africa and the Middle East.

Migration: Dispersive movements, often erratic, take place from mid-July with main movements in September and October. Some movement continues throughout the winter months with birds returning to breeding areas in March and April.

Length:	127 cm
Wing length:	38–42 cm
Weight:	♂ 3500 g, ♀ 2500 g
Call:	In flight 'kockock' or 'conk-a-conk', otherwise goose-like cackling and honking
Breeding period:	Mid-April, May, June, 1 brood per year, if all circumstances are favourable. Replacement clutch after early egg loss
Size of clutch:	1 (2) eggs
Colour of eggs:	White. Chalky deposit, discolouring them brown with continued brooding
Size of eggs:	89 × 55 mm, very variable
Incubation:	28–31 days
Fledging period:	Nidicolous; after about 10 days they form a crèche within the colony. Able to fly at 2½ months

Downy nestling in nest (one day old), Anatolia, 1970 (Wa)

Anatolia, 1970 (Wa)

Mallard (Anas platyrhynchos)

The Mallard is the most widespread of the European ducks. It is found on inland waters of all types and will tolerate human presence to the extent of living in city parks. Mallard are virtually omnivorous, taking a variety of plant material, seeds, aquatic creatures, small fish and even human leftovers. The choice of nest-site is equally varied; mostly on the ground in thick cover, but also in hollow trees, among boulders, in nest-boxes and baskets. The shallow nest is made of grass and leaves, and is lined with down. The ♀ is responsible for nest-building, incubation and care of the young, though the ♂ may assist in the early stages of incubation. The ♂ loses interest once incubation is under way and may associate with other ♀♀.

Northern and eastern populations are mostly migratory, due in part to freezing of inland waters. Western populations are more sedentary. Large flocks may occur on inland waters in winter, and sheltered coastal localities, river estuaries, etc. are also used.

Migration: Main movements in September and October with return passage in March and April. Dispersive movements take place throughout the summer.

Length:	58 cm
Wing length:	28 cm
Weight:	1100 g
Call:	'Waack, waack' or 'Wake' and 'raehb', 'quack quack quack' in diminuendo series
Breeding period:	March up to and including June, usually 1 brood per year. Repeat brood frequent
Size of clutch:	9–13 (4–18) eggs
Colour of eggs:	Pale green, blue-green to olive, very variable
Size of eggs:	58 × 41 mm
Breeding period:	24–28 days
Fledging period:	Nidifugous; able to fly at 8 weeks (end of accompaniment by parents)

oding ♀, Bavaria, 24.4.1977 (Pf)

) Ad. ♂, Bavaria, West Germany, 6.1.1976 (Pf)

♀ with young a few days old, Bavaria, 18.6.1975 (Pf)

Bavaria, 1.5.1977 (Pf)

Teal (Anas crecca)

Teal frequent most sorts of inland waters, marshes and rivers, favouring shallow water, where they can dabble for animal material ·(mostly in summer) and plant material (mostly seeds) in winter.

The nest site is on the ground in thick cover, rarely far from water. The nest is a hollow formed of grass and leaves lined with down. The ♀ is responsible for nest-building, incubation and care of the young. The species pairs in the winter quarters or on migration to the breeding areas. The ♂♂ are promiscuous and pay no attention to the ♀♀ once incubation commences.

Teal are mainly migratory, the northern and eastern populations wintering in west and southern Europe. Some birds move to North, or even tropical Africa. Flocks will inhabit sheltered coastal waters, salt-marshes and estuaries in winter.

Hard weather affects the winter distribution of birds in the Low Countries and the British Isles, and they move further west with approaching cold weather.

Migration: Main autumn movements in September–November with dispersal throughout the summer months. Return passage in March and April.

Length:	36 cm
Wing length:	18 cm
Weight:	350 g
Call:	'Crick, crick', with many variants
Breeding period:	(Beginning of April), May, June, 1 brood per year. Repeat clutch possible
Size of clutch:	8–11 (7–15) eggs
Colour of eggs:	Cream to light olive-brown
Size of eggs:	45 × 33 mm
Incubation:	21–23 days
Fledging period:	Nidifugous; able to fly at 25–30 days; young independent on fledging

♀, Bavaria, 1975 (Li)

♀ in non-breeding plumage, Bavaria, 29.8.1974 (Pf)

Seewinkel, Austria, 1962 (Li)

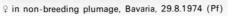

♂) ♂ on banks of the Isar, Bavaria, West Germany, 4.3.1973 (Pf)

79

Garganey (Anas querquedula)

Garganey frequent shallow inland waters with flooded meadows, marshes or other areas without dense vegetation. Food is both animal and plant matter and is obtained by swimming with the head submerged, rarely by up-ending. The pair-bond is formed in the winter quarters. The nest-site is on the ground in thick cover, usually grass or rushes. The nest is usually close to water and is a shallow cup of leaves and grass lined with down. The ♀ is entirely responsible for nest-building, incubation and care of the young. The ♂♂ will remain close to the nest during incubation, but form flocks with other ♂♂ once pair-bond ends.

Garganey are entirely migratory, being a summer visitor to Europe. A very small number winter in the Mediterranean area, but the majority make a trans-Saharan crossing to winter in tropical Africa, particularly in West Africa, where vast flocks occur.

Migration: Dispersal of the ♂♂ to form moulting flocks in June–July. Main autumn movements in mid-August to mid-October. Early migrants return in February, most in May and early April.

Length:	38 cm
Wing length:	19 cm
Weight:	320 g
Call:	♂ Rattling 'clairrrp'; also 'geck, krrt'
Breeding period:	(Mid-April) May, June (July), 1 brood per year. Repeat brood possible
Size of clutch:	8–9 (6–14) eggs
Colour of eggs:	Creamy yellow
Size of eggs:	46 × 33 mm
Incubation:	21–23 days
Fledging period:	Nidifugous; able to fly at 35–40 days when parental care ceases

♀, Bavaria, November 1977 (Li)

Ad. non-breeding ♂, Bavaria, August 1976 (Li)

Amrum, West Germany, June 1963 (Qu)

) Ad. ♂, Bavaria, West Germany, 1976 (Li)

Gadwall (Anas strepera)

Gadwall are found in shallow inland waters with plenty of cover from emergent vegetation or bankside growth. They dislike brackish or saline water, though in winter they may be found on estuaries as well as lakes, marshes and lagoons.

Food is chiefly plant material and is obtained by swimming with head submerged, more rarely by up-ending or surface feeding.

Pair-formation takes place from late summer, with most birds paired by October. The nest is a hollow of grass and reeds lined with down; it is rarely far from water. It is usually hidden in dense cover but is occasionally in the open when in association with Gulls and Terns. The ♀ builds the nest, incubates and rears the young. The pair-bond is broken at the time of egg-laying and the ♂♂ desert to form moulting flocks.

Gadwall are largely resident in the western part of their range but those breeding in the north and east migrate to the Mediterranean region, North Africa and even to tropical Africa.

Migration: The ♂♂ moult-dispersal from early June. Normal migration in October and November, returning in March and April.

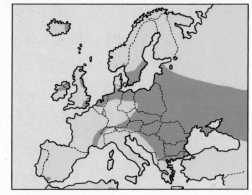

Length:	51 cm
Wing length:	27 cm
Weight:	700 g
Voice:	Courting call of ♂ 'ooii' or 'aaay' and 'zee-raeb' and a high-pitched peeping, grunting whistle. ♀ quack like Mallard
Breeding period:	End of April, May, June, 1 brood per year. Replacement clutch frequent
Size of clutch:	8–12 (6–15) eggs
Colour of eggs:	Creamy yellow
Size of eggs:	55 × 39 mm
Incubation:	24–26 days
Fledging period:	Nidifugous; able to fly at 45–50 days, when independent

, Föhr, May 1966 (Qu)

Ad. ♂, Föhr, West Germany, May 1966 (Qu)

Bavaria, West Germany, 2.1.1977 (Pf)

Camargue, France, 1967 (Li)

Wigeon (Anas penelope)

The Wigeon has a northerly distribution and is found on open areas of fresh water, avoiding dense vegetation. In winter it has a more coastal distribution, favouring salt-marshes, mudflats as well as floodland.

It is largely vegetarian and will graze on dry land as well as feeding on floating vegetation or swimming with head submerged. In winter eel-grass (*Zostera*) is an important food.

Pairing takes place in late autumn and through the winter. The ♀ builds a shallow nest of grass and leaves, lined with down, usually sited in cover under overhanging vegetation and seldom far from water. The ♀ incubates and rears the young alone.

A few Wigeon are resident but most are highly migratory, moving to coastal areas or floodlands in western Europe, the Mediterranean, North Africa and the Middle East.

Pintail (Anas acuta)

Pintail have a similar distribution to Wigeon though prefer more open water in grassland habitats. Their winter range is also similar, favouring floodlands, estuaries and inland waters.

Migration: For both species: dispersal of the ♂♂ in moulting flocks from late May. Main migration in September—November with return passage in late March to early May.

Length:	46 cm	Wigeon
Wing length:	26 cm	
Weight:	800 g	
Voice:	♂ 'whee-oo' and 'hweewee'. ♀ creaking 'terr'	
Breeding period:	May, June, 1 brood per year. Replacement clutch possible and occasional 2nd brood	
Size of clutch:	8–9 (6–12) eggs	
Colour of eggs:	Creamy yellow	
Size of eggs:	55 × 39 mm	
Incubation:	24–25 days	
Fledging period:	Nidifugous; independent at 40–50 days when able to fly	

Length:	♀ 56 cm, ♂ 66 cm Pintail
Wing length:	27 cm
Weight:	900 g
Voice:	♂ 'kryck' and 'geeeh'. ♀ creaking 'arr'
Breeding period:	Mid-April, May, June, 1 brood per year. Replacement clutch regular
Size of clutch:	7–11 (6–12) eggs
Colour of eggs:	Greeny yellow to creamy yellow
Size of eggs:	55 × 39 mm
Incubation:	22–24 days
Fledging period:	Nidifugous; able to fly at 40–45 days; then independent

r of Wigeons, Bavaria, 1975 (Li)

Pair of Pintails, Bavaria, 1975 (Li)

:) Ad. Wigeon ♀, Bavaria, West Germany, 6.3.1976 (Pf)

Shoveler (Anas clypeata)

Shoveler frequent small, shallow inland waters in lowland areas. Specialised feeding behaviour requires similar habitat in winter quarters, though brackish or saline inland waters are used. Shoveler are omnivorous, taking aquatic animals, insects and plant matter, usually surface-feeding with a sweeping motion of the bill to filter out food particles. The species will also up-end and dive for food on occasions.

The nest is sited on the ground in grass or rushes, but is more or less open. It is a shallow cup of grass and leaves lined with down, built entirely by the ♀ who also incubates and rears the young.

The pair-bond is strong, with the ♂♂ in attendance for much of the incubation period, then forming post-breeding flocks.

Shoveler are largely migratory, moving south to winter in the Mediterranean area. British birds mostly move out in winter, their place being taken by birds from Iceland or continental Europe.

Migration: The ♂♂ disperse to moult in July, main autumn migration in September to mid-November. Return passage in March and April.

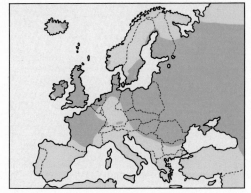

Length:	51 cm
Wing length:	24 cm
Weight:	600 g
Voice:	Courtship call of ♂ 'took-took', repeated. ♀ quacks like a Mallard
Breeding period:	(Mid-April) May, June, 1 brood per year. Replacement clutch possible
Size of clutch:	9–12 (6–14) eggs
Colour of eggs:	Pale grey-green
Size of eggs:	52 × 37 mm
Incubation:	22–25 days
Fledging period:	Nidifugous; able to fly at 40–45 days, then independent

♀, Bavaria, 28.3.1974 (Li)

♂ and ♀ in non-breeding plumage, Amrum, West Germany, October 1969 (Qu)

Föhr, West Germany, June 1968 (Qu)

↑) Ad. ♂, Bavaria, West Germany, 1976 (Li)

87

Red-crested Pochard

(Netta rufina)

The Red-crested Pochard is a bird of deep, reed-fringed lakes with open water. It also occurs on brackish lagoons and some coastal areas. The diet is mainly vegetable matter including pondweed, and is obtained by both diving and dabbling on the surface.

The nest is quite a large cup of grasses, reeds and leaves, lined with down. It is built by the ♀ and sited in dense vegetation close to the water, sometimes on floating reeds. There is a strong pair-bond with the ♂♂ in attendance near nest during incubation and sometimes remaining near to brood, though the ♀ incubates and cares for young alone.

Birds from the northern part of the range are migratory, moving to Iberia and the eastern Mediterranean in winter. Large numbers also occur in the Black and Caspian Seas, presumably Russian birds. The ♂♂ and non-breeders have a moult-migration in June, moving to favoured areas in West Germany, the Netherlands and Switzerland.

Migration: Summer moult-migration from early June. Autumn movements mostly October–November with return passage in late March and April.

Length:	♂ 56 cm, ♀ 51 cm
Wing length:	26 cm
Weight:	♂ 1000 g, ♀ 970 g
Voice:	Muted creaking or snoring noises, especially in flight
Breeding period:	End of May to mid-July, 1 brood per year. Repeat clutch possible
Size of clutch:	8–10 (6–14) eggs
Colour of eggs:	At first pale green, as incubation continues, more creamy
Size of eggs:	58 × 42 mm
Incubation:	26–28 days, beginning from last egg
Fledging period:	Nidifugous; young are able to fly at 45–50 days, when independent

ooding ♀, Bavaria, 24.4.1975 (Pf)

t) Ad. ♂, Bavaria, West Germany, 1976 (Li)

Ad. non-breeding ♂, Bavaria, 1976 (Li)

Bavaria, 1977 (Li)

89

Scaup (Aythya marila)

The Scaup is a bird of the open and wooded tundras of the North, favouring both large open waters and small pools. It feeds mainly on molluscs, insects, aquatic animals and plants.

The nest is on the ground, usually concealed in a tussock of grass, reeds or other vegetation, but sometimes in the open; it is rarely far from water. It is not colonial, but many nests may be found close together in areas of dense breeding. Nests are often found in association with colonies of gulls and terns. The ♀ is responsible for nest-building, the nest being a hollow lined with grass, reeds and down. The ♀ incubates and rears the young alone, though some ♂♂ will attend incubating ♀♀ and even accompany the brood on the water. The pair-bond is formed during the winter or early spring and generally lasts till part-way through incubation. Scaup are migratory, mainly moving to coastal waters in winter where molluscs predominate in the diet. Large numbers winter in the southern Baltic, the Firth of Forth and in the Netherlands. A few birds move further south to coasts of France and Dalmatia. Large numbers on the Black Sea are probably of Siberian origin.

Migration: Mostly late September to early November, returning in March and April.

Length:	♂ 45 cm, ♀ 40 cm
Wing length:	♂ 22 cm, ♀ 21 cm
Weight:	♂ ca 1000 g, ♀ ca 900 g
Voice:	Courting: a dove-like 'coo' and a thin whistling 'week-week-week'. Warning call: a deep harsh 'karr'
Breeding period:	May–July, 1 brood per year. Replacement clutch possible
Size of clutch:	8–11 (6–15) eggs
Colour of eggs:	Light olive-green to olive-grey; eggs resemble those of Tufted Duck
Size of eggs:	62 × 43 mm
Incubation:	24–28 days, beginning fr. laying of last egg
Fledging period:	Nidifugous; fledge at 40–45 days, when independent

♀, Zoo photograph, September 1975 (Pf)

Ad. ♂, Sweden (Ar)

Sweden, 13.7.1968 (Sy)

Ad. ♂, Zoo photograph (Li)

Tufted Duck (Aythya fuligula)

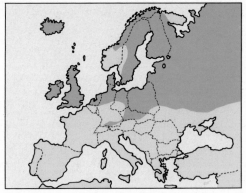

The Tufted Duck is very adaptable and is found on a variety of inland waters from lakes, ponds and rivers to parks and reservoirs. During this century it has extended its range considerably in western Europe due in part to climatic changes and also to its adaptation to man-made habitats. It is omnivorous, taking mostly plant material in summer and animal material in winter, especially molluscs.

Highly gregarious, it often nests in colonies, frequently in association with gulls and terns. The nest site, which is often on islands, is generally on the ground under cover of vegetation but occasionally in the open. The nest is a hollow of grasses, reeds and other vegetation with little down. The ♀ is solely responsible for nest-building, incubation and care of the young.

Tufted Ducks are mainly migratory, though some are resident in certain areas. Most winter in Britain and northern central Europe, some moving to Iberia, North Africa and the eastern Mediterranean. Some very long-distance movements are known, even to the Indian sub-continent, and birds of unknown origin winter in Africa.

Migration: Dispersal throughout summer. Main autumn movements in October and November, returning in late March and April.

Length:	♂ 45 cm, ♀ 43 cm
Wing length:	♂ 20.5 cm, ♀ 19.5 cm
Weight:	♂ 700 g, ♀ 650 g
Voice:	Courting ♂: a gentle 'byck, byck' or 'whee-oo', ♀ growling 'karr karr'
Breeding period:	Mid-May–July, 1 brood per year. Repeat clutch frequent
Size of clutch:	8–11 (3–22) eggs
Colour of eggs:	Matt greenish-grey, sometimes verging on brown
Size of eggs:	59 × 41 mm
Incubation:	23–25 days, beginning from last egg
Fledging period:	Nidifugous; fledge at 45–50 days, independent about that time, ♀ sometimes deserts brood from 30 days

, Bavaria, 6.2.1976 (Pf)

Ad. ♀ with young, Bavaria, 1976 (Li)

Incomplete clutch, Bavaria, 10.6.1975 (Pf)

Ad. ♂, Bavaria, West Germany (Li)

93

Pochard (Aythya ferina)

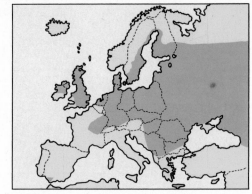

The Pochard has greatly extended its range in the last century. Originally a bird of the Asian steppes, it has now colonised much of western Europe. It is found on areas of shallow water, ranging from lakes to reservoirs and fish-ponds which have large areas of open water with reed-fringed margins. It feeds mainly on plant material, though some molluscs and other animal matter are taken, especially in winter.

The nest is situated on the ground, often in dense cover, or a floating platform of reeds may be used. The nest, of reeds, grass and lined with down, is built by the ♀ who broods and rears the young alone.

The pair-bond is of short duration, pairs being formed in the winter or more often in spring prior to mating.

Pochard are largely migratory, though some birds may be resident. Birds from eastern and northern Europe move westwards to winter on inland waters in Britain and western continental Europe. Some birds move as far as North Africa, and further large concentrations are found in south-east Europe and the Middle East.

Migration: Dispersal throughout the summer. Autumn passage in late September to November with return in March and April.

Length:	♂ 46 cm, ♀ 42 cm
Wing length:	♂ 21.5 cm, ♀ 20 cm
Weight:	♂ 850 g, ♀ 800 g
Voice:	♂ soft nasal piping; ♀ growling 'girrr' or 'quack'
Breeding period:	Beginning of May to end of July, 1 brood per year. Repeat clutch possible
Size of clutch:	8–10 (4–22) eggs
Colour of eggs:	Grey-green to cream, with matt surface
Size of eggs:	62 × 44 mm
Incubation:	24–28 days, beginning with last egg
Fledging period:	Nidifugous; able to fly at 50–55 days, independent at three weeks or at fledging

Lower Rhine, April 1977 (Gl)

Bavaria, 1977 (Li)

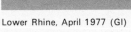

, Bavaria (Li)

Ad. ♂, Bavaria, West Germany (Li)

95

Ferruginous Duck (Aythya nyroca)

The Ferruginous Duck is found in eastern and southern Europe on shallow inland waters, rich in vegetation and fringed by dense reedbeds or other vegetation. The species differs from other *Aythya* in favouring areas with little open water. It rarely forms flocks and is often secretive and difficult to observe.

The nest is sited in reeds or other dense vegetation and is built by the ♀ of grass, reeds and leaves, lined with down. The ♂ will often remain in attendance on the brooding ♀, leaving her part-way through incubation. The Ferruginous Duck is primarily vegetarian, taking mostly seeds and aquatic plants; some aquatic insects, fish and molluscs are also taken.

The species is migratory except for southernmost breeders. Most birds move to the Mediterranean basin for the winter. Large numbers are recorded from the Black and Caspian Seas and some move to tropical Africa.

Migration: Dispersal from late August with main movements in October—November, return passage from March to May, mostly April.

Length:	♂ 42 cm, ♀ 40 cm
Wing length:	♂ 19 cm, ♀ 18 cm
Weight:	♂ 600 g, ♀ 530 g
Voice:	The soft mating calls of the ♂ sound like 'whyoo' or 'week week'. ♀ grating 'gerr gerr'
Breeding period:	Mid-May to July, 1 brood per year. Repeat clutch possible
Size of clutch:	8–10 (6–14) eggs
Colour of eggs:	Beige or reddish yellow-brown, matt or with a dull sheen
Size of eggs:	52 × 38 mm
Incubation:	25–27 days, from completion of clutch
Fledging period:	Nidifugous; able to fly at 55–60 days

and ♀, East Holstein, West Germany, 1967 (Qu)

Ad. ♂ bathing (Li)

Anatolia, 1973 (Li)

Ad. ♂, Bavaria, West Germany (Li)

Goldeneye (Bucephala clangula)

The Goldeneye is primarily a bird of the Arctic coniferous zone. It frequents lakes, pools and rivers where it feeds mainly on molluscs, crustaceans and insect larvae. It is an accomplished diver and underwater swimmer, even turning over stones under water to search for food. It has specialised breeding requirements, nesting in holes in trees or occasionally in rabbit burrows. It uses nest-boxes readily and the provision of boxes has resulted in an expansion of its range where natural nest-sites are scarce. Nesting materials are not used as such, the eggs being surrounded with down. Pair-formation starts in winter or early spring. The ♂♂ have a complex display and are aggressive towards other ♂♂.

Goldeneye are migratory and winter on both fresh and salt water. Large numbers are found in the southern Baltic, the lakes of central Europe, the British Isles and the Black Sea coasts.

Migration: Main autumn movements in October to mid-December, with return passage in late March and April.

The similar Barrow's Goldeneye (*Bucephala islandica*) is confined to Iceland within Europe, where Goldeneye are absent.

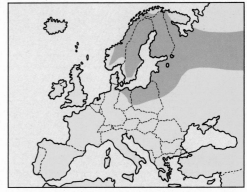

Length:	♂ 45 cm, ♀ 41 cm
Wing length:	♂ 22 cm, ♀ 20 cm
Weight:	♂ 850 g, ♀ 750 g
Voice:	Mating call of ♂ a loud 'zee-zeee' and soft 'rrrt', ♀ a deep 'grarr grarr', distinctive whistling noise from the wings in flight
Breeding period:	Beginning of April to June, 1 brood per year. Repeat clutch possible but rare
Size of clutch:	8–11 (5–13) eggs
Colour of eggs:	Freshly laid eggs are blue-green, paling later
Size of eggs:	60 × 42 mm
Incubation:	27–32 days, as soon as clutch complete
Fledging period:	Nidifugous; able to fly at 57–66 days

, with Tufted Duck, Schleswig-Holstein, West
…any (Ar)
Goldeneye displaying, zoo photograph, 4.4.1972 (Pf)

♀ with chicks, Hammerdal, Sweden, July 1977 (Di)

Clutch in nest box, Schleswig-Holstein (Sy)

Long-tailed Duck (Clangula hyemalis)

The Long-tailed Duck is an inhabitant of the high Arctic tundra. Breeding on pools or small islets off the coast, it shows a dislike of flowing water. It is an outstanding diver, feeding on crustaceans and molluscs, as well as small fish, insects and some plant matter.

It nests on the ground in cover of scrub or other vegetation, sometimes in rock-crevices; the nest is rarely far from water. Nests are usually solitary, though loose colonies are known, especially in association with nesting terns. There is little nesting material, the eggs being surrounded by down.

The ♀ broods and rears the young alone. Sometimes the ♀ will desert the brood after hatching and a small crèche may be formed under the care of other ♀♀.

The species is mainly migratory, moving to coastal waters in winter, where large flocks are formed, particularly in the Baltic. Other large concentrations are found off the coasts of Scotland, Norway and Iceland. The habit of wintering in large flocks means that they are particularly susceptible to oil-pollution.

Migration: Main autumn movement in October—November, with return in April and May.

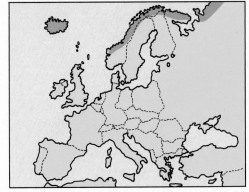

Length:	♂ 56 cm, ♀ 41 cm; tail 21 cm (. 6.5 cm)
Wing length:	♂ 22 cm, ♀ 21 cm
Weight:	♂ 770 g, ♀ 600 g
Voice:	Courting: ♂ 'a-a-aoow-gah', loud and far-carrying. ♀ 'urk' or 'ved'
Breeding period:	End of May to July, 1 brood per year. Repeat clutch possible
Size of clutch:	5–9 (4–11) eggs, more resulting fr. 2 ♀♀
Colour of eggs:	Yellowish to olive-grey, sometimes greenish
Size of eggs:	54 × 38 mm
Incubation:	24–29 days, commencing with last egg
Fledging period:	Nidifugous; fledge at 35–40 days when independent

in summer plumage, Sweden (Ar)

Ad. ♂ in summer plumage (Gé)

♀ with young (Gé)

Ad. ♂ in winter plumage, Amrum, West Germany, February 1970 (Qu)

Velvet Scoter (Melanitta fusca)

The Velvet Scoter breeds in taiga, wooded tundra and on offshore islets and skerries. The nest is usually on the ground in thick vegetation, low scrub or grass, and it will occasionally use nest-boxes. Nest-building is done by the ♀ using grass, small twigs and lined with down. The ♂ usually deserts the ♀ in the latter part of incubation but will sometimes remain to defend the ♀ and her brood. The food is chiefly molluscs, though small crabs and occasionally small fish are also taken. In winter the species is maritime and is found along the coasts of Norway, the southern Baltic, Kattegat and in smaller numbers off the British and north French coasts.

The **Common Scoter** (*Melanitta nigra*) is found on tundra and other open habitat. The nest is often far from water and is constructed by the ♀ from grass, moss and down. It is usually concealed under vegetation. The ♂ deserts the ♀ after incubation commences and the ♀ broods and rears the young alone. The diet is made up of molluscs, insect larvae, fish eggs and some vegetable matter. In winter the Common Scoter is largely marine, being found off the coasts of Britain, Norway, the Kattegat and the southern Baltic. Some birds move much further south and the species is common off the coasts of Iberia and the Atlantic coast of north-west Africa.

Migration: Similar for both species. Autumn movements mostly October–November, returning in April and May. Both species have a moult-migration: the Velvet Scoter to the Kattegat and the Common Scoter to Jutland.

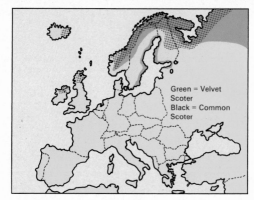

Green = Velvet Scoter
Black = Common Scoter

Length:	♂ 56 cm, ♀ 50 cm Velvet Scoter
Wing length:	♂ 28 cm, ♀ 26 cm
Weight:	♂ 1600 g, ♀ 1500 g
Voice:	Has few calls: courting: ♂ 'vak-vak', ♀ vibrating 'braaa-braaa-braaa'
Breeding period:	End of May to July, 1 brood per year. Repeat clutch possible
Size of clutch:	7–10 (6–11) eggs
Colour of eggs:	Cream to light brown, matt surface
Size of eggs:	73 × 48 mm
Incubation:	27–28 days; begins when clutch complete
Fledging period:	Nidifugous; abandoned by ♀ at 4–5 weeks. Able to fly at 7–8 weeks

Common Scoter ad. ♂, Amrum, West Germany, February 1972 (Qu)

Common Scoter ♀ with chicks (Gé)

et Scoter ♂, Aland, Finland, May 1974 (Di)

) Velvet Scoter brooding (Gé)

103

Eider (Somateria mollissima)

The Eider is a sea duck found along the shallower coasts of northern Europe. It feeds largely upon molluscs, crustaceans and other marine creatures and is obtained by surface-diving.

Eider are very gregarious throughout the year. Nests are often in colonies of up to 3000 pairs, though solitary nests are frequent. It will often associate with colonies of terns. The nest is a hollow lined with large quantities of down. The ♀ broods and rears the young alone, though the ♂♂ will stand guard during the early stages of incubation. The ♂♂ and non-breeders form large moulting flocks during the summer. The young are often gathered together in large crèches.

Eider form pairs in late autumn through to early spring. The ♂♂ are extremely vocal and there is a great deal of display within the flocks.

Migration: Partially migratory. The ♂♂ and non-breeders form moulting flocks in summer often in certain areas. Baltic breeding birds move to the Jutland coast and the Waddensee. British birds are largely resident, perhaps moving up to 200 km to areas where food is abundant. Longer movements are known, and some birds move to the Channel coasts of France and England.

Length:	58 cm
Wing length:	♂ 30 cm
Weight:	♂ 2250 g, ♀ 1900 g
Voice:	♂ a resonant 'aa-ooo' or 'ow ow'; ♀ deep 'goggoggogg' or growling 'krok'
Breeding period:	End of April to end of June, 1 brood per year. Repeat clutch possible
Size of clutch:	4–6 (2–8) eggs
Colour of eggs:	Variable, greenish-grey or beige to olive-green, with a matt sheen
Size of eggs:	76 × 52 mm
Incubation:	25–28 days, starting from complete clutch
Fledging period:	Nidifugous; independent at 55–60 days, fledged by 75 days

♂ wintering in Bavaria, West Germany, 16.1.1974
Zoo photograph (Li)

♀ with crèche of young, Amrum, West Germany, June 1972 (Qu)

Amrum, May 1973 (Qu)

Red-breasted Merganser

(Mergus serrator)

The Red-breasted Merganser is found on inland and coastal waters in northern Europe. It feeds mainly on fish, obtained by diving in fairly shallow waters.

The nest is on the ground amongst tree-roots, hollows, short burrows and rocks, or concealed in vegetation, and is a hollow lined with grass, leaves and down. The ♀ takes care of nest-building, incubation and rearing the young. The ♂♂ usually desert the ♀♀ during incubation but are occasionally seen with the ♀♀ and young.

The pair-bond is formed during the winter or in early spring, the ♂♂ and non-breeders forming moulting-flocks in summer.

In winter the species is largely marine, though it also occurs on reservoirs and other large inland waters particularly in central Europe. Some birds perform a moult-migration with large numbers recorded off the Danish coast. It is very widespread in winter, some birds remaining in Icelandic or Norwegian waters, while others move south to the Channel coasts, the Atlantic coast of France and even to the Mediterranean. Birds, presumably of eastern populations, winter on the Black and Caspian Seas.

Migration: Movements to moulting areas from early June. In autumn, main movements in October—November, with return in late March to early May.

Length:	♂ 58 cm, ♀ 54 cm
Wing length:	♂ 24 cm, ♀ 22 cm
Weight:	♂ 1100 g, ♀ 900 g
Voice:	♂ hoarse 'yeow' or 'grah', ♀ rattling 'garr' and 'rok rok rok'
Breeding period:	Mid-May to July, 1 brood per year. Repeat clutch possible
Size of clutch:	5–10 (–15) eggs, larger cl. result of two ♀♀
Colour of eggs:	Cream, light brown or olive-green
Size of eggs:	64 × 45 mm
Incubation:	29–35 days, from complete clutch
Fledging period:	Nidifugous; able to fly at ca 60–65 days. Crèches formed where species numerous

eswig-Holstein (Ar)

) Ad. ♂ (foreground), ♀ behind, Schleswig-Holstein, West Germany (Ar)

Red-breasted Mergansers courting, south coast of Finland, May 1969 (Willy)

♂, Aland, Finland, May 1974 (Wö)

107

Goosander (Mergus merganser)

The Goosander frequents inland waters ranging from fast-flowing rivers to large lakes. Unlike the Red-breasted Merganser, it is rarely seen on marine waters. It feeds largely on fish, though other aquatic creatures such as crustaceans and insects are also taken.

The nest-site is usually in a hole in a tree, or in a bank or amongst rocks; it frequently uses nest-boxes. The nest is usually near water but may be up to 1 km away. Little nesting material is used other than down.

The pair-bond is formed during the winter or early spring and the ♂♂ desert the ♀♀ during incubation. The ♀ broods and rears the young alone, and may leave the young before they fledge.

The species is gregarious outside the breeding season with large flocks wintering on suitable waters. Some populations are largely resident whilst others migrate to winter in southern England and much of northern Continental Europe. Large concentrations are found in the Black and Caspian Seas.

Migration: Moult-migration not fully understood but may involve some long-distance movements. Autumn migration mainly October and November with return in late March to early May.

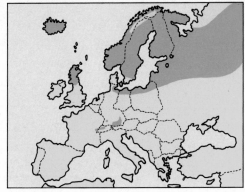

Length:	♂ 66 cm, ♀ 58 cm
Wing length:	♂ 28 cm, ♀ 26 cm
Weight:	♂ 1600 g, ♀ 1400 g
Voice:	♂ Metallic sounds like 'ker-kor, ker-ker-kor'. ♀ a quacking 'kokokokok' or 'eck-eck'
Breeding period:	Mid-May to July, 1 brood per year. Repeat clutch possible
Size of clutch:	8–12 (4–22) eggs
Colour of eggs:	Cream, smooth, and slightly shiny surface
Size of eggs:	68 × 47 mm
Incubation:	30–32 days, from laying of last egg
Fledging period:	Nidifugous; young remain up to 2 days in nest. Able to fly at ca 2 months

♂, Lech, Bavaria, 4.5.1970 (Wi)

Moosburg Reservoir, West Germany, February 1978 (Pf)

Clutch in nesting-box, Bavaria, 1970 (Li)

) ♀ with chicks, tributary of the Isar, Bavaria, West Germany, 10.6.1973 (Pf)

Smew (Mergus albellus)

The Smew is an inhabitant of the northern coniferous zone, preferring lakes and slow-flowing rivers. It feeds mainly on fish during the winter and spring and on insects at other times. The nest is normally a hole in a tree, often those made by the Black Woodpecker (*Dryocopus martius*), but it will readily use nest-boxes. There is little nesting material other than down. The pair-bond is formed in winter or more often in early spring. The ♂♂ desert the ♀♀ during incubation.

It is gregarious in winter and feeding flocks of up to 700 birds occur in suitable areas. It is rarely found on salt water, preferring inland lakes. The species is entirely migratory, wintering mainly from the southern Baltic and countries bordering the North Sea through central and eastern Europe down to the Black and Caspian Seas.

Migration: September—December, mainly October—November returning in late February to June, mostly late March to mid-May.

Length:	♂ 44 cm, ♀ 40 cm
Wing length:	♂ 20 cm, ♀ 18 cm
Weight:	*ca* 600 g
Voice:	♂ a grating 'krr-eck', 'krr'; ♀ monosyllabic 'wok'
Breeding period:	Mid-May to early July, 1 brood per year
Size of clutch:	6—9 (5—11) eggs
Colour of eggs:	Cream to beige, smooth surface
Size of eggs:	53 × 38 mm
Incubation:	26—28 days
Fledging period:	Nidifugous; able to fly at *ca* 10 weeks

Smews (Goosander second from right), Schleswig-Holstein (Ar)

vintering in Bavaria, West Germany (Se)

) ♂ and ♀ Smew, Schleswig-Holstein, West Germany (Ar)

Shelduck (Tadorna tadorna)

The Shelduck frequents coastal and brackish waters with sand or mud banks. It feeds on aquatic invertebrates, mainly molluscs, insects and crustaceans, by surface-dabbling in shallow water or on exposed wet mud. The nest is sited in a hole, and often rabbit-burrows are used. The nest-chamber is lined with down and incubation is by the ♀ only. After incubation both parents lead the brood to the water and remain with the young till the adults move away to moult. Large crèches may result when the adults leave.

Most of the north European population migrate to the Waddensee off the German coast to moult, though some gather in south-west England.

The species is both resident and migratory, depending on the population, many birds returning to their breeding areas after moult. Others, of eastern origin, winter along the North Sea and Channel coasts. Some birds move to the Mediterranean or North African coasts and others to the Black Sea.

Migration: Moult-migration in late June—August. Autumn dispersal in October—November, with return passage in March and April.

Length:	♂ 66 cm, ♀ 61 cm
Wing length:	♂ 33 cm, ♀ 30 cm
Weight:	♂ 1200 g, ♀ 800 g
Voice:	Courting: ♂ a whistling 'siurrr', 'coosiurr' or 'ju-ju-ju'; ♀ a nasal 'ak-ak-ak'
Breeding period:	End of April to end of July, 1 brood per year
Size of clutch:	7—12 eggs
Colour of eggs:	Cream, with a matt sheen
Size of eggs:	66 × 47 mm
Incubation:	29—31 days
Fledging period:	Nidifugous; able to fly at 5—6 weeks

of Shelduck, central Anatolia, 2.6.1974 (Pf)

) Ad. ♂, Anatolia, 1974 (Li)

Chicks, Norderney, North Sea, July 1975 (Di)

Clutch in a heap of straw, Amrum, West Germany, June 1967 (Qu)

Ruddy Shelduck (Tadorna ferruginea)

The Ruddy Shelduck frequents brackish, fresh and inland salt waters. Though coastal in some areas, it also frequents mountainous country and even desert areas. It is omnivorous, feeding mostly on plant material, but also on invertebrates. It will feed on land, taking young shoots and grain, as well as in shallow water.

The nest-sites are very varied: holes, either natural or sometimes excavated by other animals, in buildings, hollow trees, on cliff-ledges, in nest-boxes and even in abandoned nests of birds of prey. The nest is just a hollow lined with down and the ♀ incubates alone. Both parents take care of the young and remain with them till fledging.

The species is dispersive and nomadic though some birds migrate. The winter habitat differs little from that used during the breeding season. Large numbers winter in Turkey and parts of the Middle East, some birds from North Africa move to south-west Spain, the only instance of a species which nests in Africa migrating to Europe to winter. Sometimes it occurs north of its breeding range but there are many records of it in Britain and in other north European countries due to escapes.

Migration: Dispersal from August, mostly September—November returning in March and April.

Length:	♂ 63 cm, ♀ 60 cm
Wing length:	♂ 36 cm, ♀ 33 cm
Weight:	♂ 1300 g, ♀ 1100 g
Voice:	Noisy, nasal calls, 'ang', 'a-honk'; ♀ 'ka-ha-ha'
Breeding period:	Mid-April to June, 1 brood per year
Size of clutch:	8–13 (–16) eggs
Colour of eggs:	Dirty white, with a matt sheen
Size of eggs:	67 × 47 mm
Incubation:	28–29 days
Fledging period:	Nidifugous; fledge at about 55 days, independent soon after

ft), ♂ (right) with young, with Slender-billed Gull ckground, Anatolia 1973 (Zei) ♀ (foreground) and ♂ (behind)

Bavaria, 25.8.1968 (Li)

Ad. ♀♀ seeking food, Bavaria, West Germany, 25.8.1968 (Li)

115

Greylag Goose (Anser anser)

The Greylag Goose frequents a wide variety of habitats ranging from arctic tundra to marshlands, reedbeds and islands in large lakes. Its range has decreased considerably due to drainage and loss of habitat, though reintroduction accounts for some recent spread. It nests on the ground among reeds, low vegetation such as heather or in sheltered hollows. The nest is a large structure, which may be used in successive years, made of available plant materials and lined with down. The species is monogamous and birds normally pair for life. The ♀ incubates alone but the ♂ guards the site and both parents take care of the young.

The food is entirely vegetable material, and includes aquatic plants, grasses, seeds and crops such as potatoes, turnips and cereals.

Outside the breeding season the species is highly gregarious, forming large flocks on migration and in areas where food is abundant. In winter it frequents agricultural land with crops or stubble fields, marshes and open grasslands, often roosting in large concentrations on lakes, mudflats or marshes.

Most populations are migratory, Icelandic birds moving to Britain, Scandinavian and north-east European birds to France and Spain. Other populations winter in south-east Europe and parts of the Middle East and North Africa.

Migration: Main autumn movements from late September to November, returning in February and March.

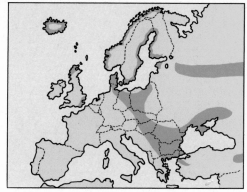

Length:	♂ 89 cm, ♀ 76 cm
Wing length:	♂ 46 cm, ♀ 44 cm
Weight:	♂ 3400 g, ♀ 3000 g
Voice:	A clattering nasal 'aang-ung-ung' or trumpeting sounds
Breeding period:	End of March to June, 1 brood per year. Repeat clutch possible
Size of clutch:	4–6 (3–12) eggs
Colour of eggs:	Dirty white, without gloss
Size of eggs:	86 × 57 mm
Incubation:	27–28 days, from complete clutch
Fledging period:	Nidifugous; able to fly at *ca* 9 weeks. Young remain with parents through winter

nau. Austria, 5.10.1971 (Wi)

Ad. Greylag Geese, naturalised in Austria, 1975 (Li)

♀ with newly hatched young, Amrum, West Germany, May 1974 (Qu)

Schleswig-Holstein, West Germany, 26.4.1975 (Sy)

117

White-fronted Goose

(Anser albifrons)

The White-fronted Goose is a high-arctic bird, frequenting the tundra zone for breeding. It is highly migratory and winters in Britain and Ireland, the Low Countries and in eastern and south-east Europe.

Lesser White-fronted Goose (Anser erythropus)

This small goose is a rare breeding bird in northern Europe. It is found on the edges of wooded tundra, mountain slopes and boggy areas. It nests on hummocks or rocky outcrops, usually in the open but sometimes in scrub. The nest is lined with grass and down and may be used in successive years. The ♂ stands guard on the incubating ♀ and both parents share in the care of the young. The food is mainly shoots of tundra plants, grasses and sedges.

The species is migratory, wintering in small numbers in south-east Europe and parts of the Middle East. Stragglers sometimes reach western Europe, usually in flocks of White-fronted Geese.

Migration: Similar for both species. Autumn passage from September mainly October—December. Spring movements in late March to May.

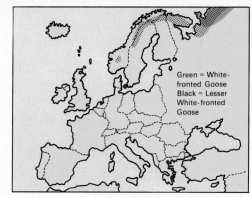

Green = White-fronted Goose
Black = Lesser White-fronted Goose

Length:	♂ 76 cm, ♀ 66 cm White-fronted Goose
Wing length:	♂ 42 cm, ♀ 40 cm
Weight:	♂ 2400 g, ♀ 2100 g
Voice:	Metallic, usually disyllabic calls, 'ki-lick', 'cow-lyow'
Breeding period:	Mid-June to July, 1 brood per year
Size of clutch:	5–6 (3–7) eggs
Colour of eggs:	Yellowish white, smooth-shelled with slight sheen
Size of eggs:	79 × 52 mm
Incubation:	27–28 days, from complete clutch
Fledging period:	Nidifugous; able to fly at ca 40 days, young remain with parents during winter

Length:	♂ 66 cm, ♀ 53 cm Lesser White-fronted
Wing length:	♂ 38 cm, ♀ 37 cm
Weight:	♂ 2100 g, ♀ 1900 g
Voice:	Higher than that of White-fronted Goose and more rapid, 'kow-yow', 'tyoo-yoo-yoo'
Breeding period:	End of May to end of July, 1 brood per year
Size of clutch:	4–5 (3–8) eggs
Colour of eggs:	Yellowish white, with a dull gleam
Size of eggs:	76 × 49 mm
Incubation:	25–28 days, beginning from last egg
Fledging period:	Nidifugous; young can fly at ca 5 weeks, remain with parents through winter

er Rhine, West Germany, January 1976 (Gl)

Pair of White-fronted Geese (Li)

Lesser White-fronted Goose, zoo photograph (Pa)

Bean Goose (Anser fabalis)

The Bean Goose has several distinct races, some with marked differences in choice of habitat. The race which breeds in Scandinavia (*fabalis*) nests in dense forest of conifers or birch scrub, moving to tundra for a short period after nesting. The nest-site is usually a hummock close to water or at the base of a tree or among bushes. The nest is a mound of grass and other plant matter lined with down. The ♀ broods alone but the ♂ defends the territory. The species is monogamous and normally pairs for life.

The food is entirely plant matter, including grasses, seeds, cereal crops, roots and berries.

Bean Geese are gregarious outside the breeding season and frequent agricultural land, steppes and flooded grassland. Only small numbers winter in Britain, the main wintering areas being countries bordering the Baltic and southern North Sea, and through central and eastern Europe. Small numbers also occur in France and Iberia.

Migration: September–November, though birds wintering in Britain arrive in January. Return passage in March and April into May.

Pink-footed Goose (Anser brachyrhynchus)

This species breeds in Iceland and the high Arctic. It winters in Britain, the Low Countries and Denmark.

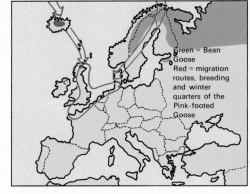

Green = Bean Goose
Red = migration routes, breeding and winter quarters of the Pink-footed Goose

Length:	♂ 82 cm, ♀ 66 cm Bean Goose
Wing length:	♂ 48 cm, ♀ 46 cm
Weight:	♂ 3100 g, ♀ 2800 g
Voice:	In flight, a deep trumpeting 'ka-yack' or 'ung-ank'
Breeding period:	End of May to July, 1 brood per year, probably no repeat clutch
Size of clutch:	4–6 (3–8) eggs
Colour of eggs:	White, becoming very dirty as brooding progresses
Size of eggs:	83 × 55 mm
Incubation:	27–29 days, from complete clutch
Fledging period:	Nidifugous; able to fly at *ca* 40 days. Young remain with parents through winter

Length:	♂ 76 cm, ♀ 61 cm Pink-footed Goose
Wing length:	♂ 45 cm, ♀ 42 cm
Weight:	♂ 2700 g, ♀ 2450 g
Voice:	Flight call higher than that of *A.f. fabalis*, 'ang-ank' or 'king-wink'
Breeding period:	Mid-May to July, 1 brood per year, no replacement clutch
Size of clutch:	3–5 (1–9) eggs
Colour of eggs:	White to yellowish white, with a dull sheen
Size of eggs:	78 × 53 mm
Incubation:	26–27 days, from complete clutch
Fledging period:	Nidifugous; able to fly at *ca* 8 weeks, but remain in family group until next breeding season

a Bean Goose (*A.f. rossicus*) (Ar)

Pink-footed Goose, Schleswig-Holstein, West Germany (Ar)

Pair of Bean Geese, Föhr, West Germany, May 1972 (Qu)

Brent Goose (Branta bernicla)

The Brent Goose is a bird of the high Arctic tundras. It nests colonially, the nests being sited on dry hummocks in the tundra or on small islets in rivers or off the coast. The nest is a shallow depression lined with moss, lichens and down, built by the ♀ who incubates alone, the ♂ standing guard and helping to rear the brood.

It feeds on plant materials: in summer on tundra plants, mosses and lichens. In winter it is largely coastal feeding on Zostera, marine algae and salt-marsh plants as well as on grass and young wheat.

There are three discrete populations: *bernicla*, the dark-bellied form, breeds in the USSR and winters from Denmark to Northern France and south-east England. The light-bellied race *hrota* breeds in Greenland and the Canadian Arctic islands and winters in Ireland and north-west France. Another population of *hrota* breeds in Spitzbergen and Franz Josef Land, wintering mainly in Denmark, though some move to north-east England in hard weather.

Migration: Autumn migration in mid-September to November, return passage in late March to June.

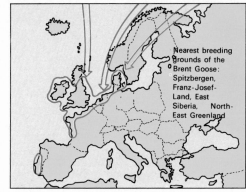

Nearest breeding grounds of the Brent Goose: Spitzbergen, Franz-Josef-Land, East Siberia, North-East Greenland

Length:	♂ 60 cm, ♀ 56 cm
Wing length:	♂ 34 cm, ♀ 33 cm
Weight:	♂ 1600 g, ♀ 1250 g
Voice:	Deep monosyllabic calls, 'cronk' or 'rott-rott'
Breeding period:	From beginning of June, 1 brood per year
Size of clutch:	3–5 (2–8) eggs
Colour of eggs:	Whitish grey, becoming dirtier as brooding progresses
Size of eggs:	74 × 47 mm
Incubation:	24–26 days
Fledging period:	Nidifugous; young remain in family group until next breeding season

m, May 1955 (Qu)

Amrum, Schleswig-Holstein, West Germany, May 1975 (Qu)

Brent geese migrating, Amrum, May 1968 (Qu)

Canada Goose (Branta canadensis)

The Canada Goose was introduced into England from North America in the seventeenth century. Further introductions in Britain and Ireland as well as in Norway, Sweden and other European countries have resulted in the species becoming naturalised and expanding its range beyond that of the initial introductions. It is found on lakes, pools and ornamental waters especially where grassy banks offer good feeding. The nest-site is usually close to water, often at the base of a tree or on islands where present. The species is colonial, though solitary nests occur. The nest is a mound of grass, reeds and other plant material lined with down. Incubation is by the ♀ alone though the ♂ stands guard.

The Canada Goose feeds mainly on plant matter including some aquatic plants. Most of the food is taken on land where shoots, roots, cereals and seeds form the diet.

The British population is largely resident, though there is a strong moult-migration, particularly from Yorkshire to Invernesshire. Scandinavian breeders move to Germany and the Netherlands in winter. Some wild Canada Geese from North America occur in very small numbers in Ireland and west Scotland in winter.

Migration: Main movements in mid September to November and return in late February to April.

Length:	♂ 99 cm, ♀ 94 cm
Wing length:	♂ 49 cm, ♀ 47 cm
Weight:	♂ 4900 g, ♀ 4400 g
Voice:	Loud and penetrating 'ah-honk', rising in pitch on second syllable
Breeding period:	End of March to June, 1 brood per year. Repeat clutch rare
Size of clutch:	4–6 (2–11) eggs
Colour of eggs:	Yellowish white, lustreless
Size of eggs:	86 × 58 mm
Incubation:	28–30 days
Fledging period:	Nidifugous; able to fly at 40–48 days. Young remain with parents through winter

...oding, Bavaria, 5.5.1963 (Pf)

...Bavaria, West Germany, 1976 (Li)

♂ and ♀ with chicks (Ar)

Mute Swan (Cygnus olor)

The Mute Swan was introduced into many west-European countries though wild stock was present in eastern Europe and Britain. About 30 years ago the species was scarce in many areas but, due to protection and introductions, it is now extremely common over much of its range. The species is found on lakes, slow-flowing rivers, ornamental waters and in parks. Due to mixtures of feral and wild stock the species is very tolerant of man except in eastern Europe. The nest is a huge structure of reeds and other aquatic vegetation usually on banks, islands or in reed-beds. It is built by both sexes. The ♀ incubates alone though the ♂ will take over during feeding periods. The food is mainly aquatic vegetation, leaves of waterside plants and some shoots and other plant material taken on land.

The species is markedly territorial and the ♂ is often very aggressive in defence of the nest. Despite this behaviour, some colonies are known where nests may be close together.

Though resident over much of its range, the northern European populations are migratory, moving to coastal areas of the southern Baltic, Denmark and Germany. Further movements may occur in hard weather to central Europe.

Migration: Autumn movements mainly October–December, returning in March.

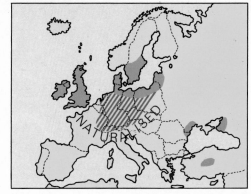

Length:	♂ 159 cm, ♀ 155 cm
Wing length:	♂ 61 cm, ♀ 57 cm
Weight:	10,000–20,000 g
Voice:	Mostly silent but some gurgling and trumpeting sounds, hissing when threatened
Breeding period:	Mid-April to June, 1 brood per year. Repeat clutch possible
Size of clutch:	5–8 (4–11) eggs
Colour of eggs:	White to grey-green, turning a dirty brown
Size of eggs:	114 × 74 mm
Incubation:	35–38 days, from complete clutch
Fledging period:	Nidifugous; able to fly at ca 4½ months. Young remain with parents through winter

Day-old chicks, Bavaria, 10.5.1977 (Pf)

Bavaria, 24.4.1977 (Pf)

aria, 12.4.1977 (Pf)

) Winter gathering on Kochelsee, Bavaria, West Germany, 1975 (Li)

Whooper Swan (Cygnus cygnus)

The Whooper Swan is found on lakes and pools in tundra as well as shallow reed-fringed lakes and other wetland further south. The nest is usually sited on an island or promontory and is a substantial mound of reeds or other plant matter and a little down. It is built by the ♀ from material passed to her by the ♂. The ♀ incubates alone, though the ♂ may take over in her absence. Both parents share in the care of the young. The food is entirely plant matter, mostly aquatic vegetation, though there is an increasing tendency to graze on land.

The Icelandic population mostly migrates to Britain and Ireland, though some are resident. The Scandinavian and USSR birds move to Baltic coasts, Germany and the Netherlands as well as to south-east Europe and the Black and Caspian Seas.

Autumn migration occurs in late September to November, returning in late March to May.

The smaller **Bewick's Swan** (*Cygnus columbianus*) breeds only in the high Arctic tundra. It winters in Britain and Ireland, and from France to Denmark. It has a similar migration pattern to the Whooper Swan, though passage continues into June in high latitudes.

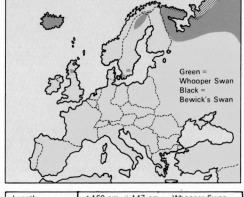

Green = Whooper Swan
Black = Bewick's Swan

Length:	♂ 160 cm, ♀ 147 cm	Whooper Swan
Wing length:	♂ 61 cm, ♀ 58 cm	
Weight:	5000–10,700 g	
Voice:	Loud trumpeting 'ang-ha' (in flight), otherwise monosyllabic 'ang' or 'huck'; very vocal	
Breeding period:	End of April to June, 1 brood per year	
Size of clutch:	3–5 (–8) eggs	
Colour of eggs:	Yellowish white to bluish, with a grainy surface	
Size of eggs:	113 × 74 mm	
Incubation:	*ca* 35 days, beginning fr. complete clutch	
Fledging period:	Nidifugous; able to fly at *ca* 2½ months. Young remain with parents through winter	

Length:	♂ 125 cm, ♀ 116 cm	Bewick's Swan
Wing length:	♂ 52 cm, ♀ 50 cm	
Weight:	♂ 6500 g, ♀ 5200 g	
Voice:	High pitched 'bong' in flight, also 'couk' and 'hog-og-og', very vocal	
Breeding period:	Late May to July, 1 brood per year	
Size of clutch:	3–5 (2–6) eggs	
Colour of eggs:	Yellowish white, with a dull sheen	
Size of eggs:	102 × 68 mm	
Incubation:	29–30 days	
Fledging period:	Nidifugous; able to fly at 40–50 days. Young remain with parents through winter	

ooper Swans, Sweden (Ar)

Whooper Swan (behind), Bewick's Swan (foreground), Schleswig-Holstein, West Germany (Sou)

t) Whooper Swan ♀ on clutch, zoo photograph, May 1974 (Pf)

Egyptian Vulture

(Neophron percnopterus)

In Europe the Egyptian Vulture is found mainly in warm, Mediterranean countries frequenting rocky or mountainous habitat for nesting. It feeds on carrion of all types, as well as human refuse, small mammals and birds, some of which may be taken alive. It makes lengthy searching flights for food and will concentrate in areas where food is plentiful. Pairs are formed after a spectacular aerial display. The nest site is usually on a cliff ledge or cave, sometimes on old buildings or trees. The nest is a pile of branches lined with rubbish including paper, wool, bones, rags, etc. Incubation is by both sexes and both take part in rearing the young. Though nests are solitary, large gatherings may occur at suitable feeding sites and at roosts.

Most of the European population is migratory, though some may remain in Iberia, France or the Balkans. The species avoids a long crossing of the Mediterranean by concentrating at the Bosphorus and at Gibraltar. Most winter just south of the Sahara.

Migration: Autumn movements from late July, mostly late August to mid-September. Spring passage from March to May.

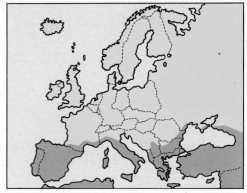

Length:	60–70 cm
Wing length:	50 cm
Weight:	2200 g
Voice:	Adults mostly mute; soft hissing and grunting when excited
Breeding period:	April to beginning of June, 1 brood per year. Replacement clutch possible
Size of clutch:	2 (1–3) eggs
Colour of eggs:	From almost pure white to chocolate brown
Size of eggs:	66 × 50 mm
Incubation:	ca 42 days, incubating from first egg
Fledging period:	Nidicolous; able to fly at 2.5–3 months

ptian Vultures with carrion, Anatolia, 1975 (Li)

Anatolia, 21.5.1974 (Pf)

Macedonia, Yugoslavia, 1970 (Li)

) Ad. in eyrie with young, Anatolia, Turkey, 24.5.1974 (Pf)

131

Griffon Vulture (Gyps fulvus)

The Griffon Vulture breeds on cliff-ledges and caves in rocky or mountainous country. It ranges over a wide variety of habitats in aerial food searches, taking advantage of thermal air-currents. The species is colonial, nesting in groups of up to a hundred pairs. The nests, which are returned to each year, are constructed of twigs, leaves and grass. Both sexes share incubation and care of the chick.

The food consists of carrion, mainly large domestic animals. The birds are attracted to a feeding site by observation of other vultures.

Due to poisoning, both deliberate and accidental, and to improved stock management the species has declined in range and numbers throughout Europe.

Though birds from the Iberian population are largely resident there is some migration of birds from eastern Europe and Turkey, though the wintering areas are not known due to the small numbers involved. Young birds may disperse from the breeding areas, those in Iberia usually moving further west or south. Some birds occur north of their range, particularly in the Austrian Alps, where small numbers of non-breeders summer.

Migration: September—November, return in February—May.

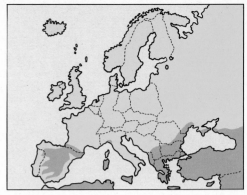

Length:	100 cm
Wing length:	♂ 72 cm, ♀ 75
Weight:	7800 g
Voice:	Chattering and hissing when excited: 'Tetetet'
Breeding period:	Mid-February to beginning of May, 1 brood per year. Replacement clutch possible
Size of clutch:	1 egg
Colour of egg:	White, sometimes with red-brown patches at one end
Size of egg:	90 × 70 mm
Incubation:	47—54 days
Fledging period:	Nidicolous; able to fly at ca 110 days

on guard at eyrie, Macedonia, 1972 (Li)

Macedonia, 1972 (Li)

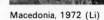

Macedonia, 1972 (Li)

) Ad. on eyrie with juv., Macedonia, Yugoslavia, 1972 (Li)

Black Vulture (Aegypius monachus)

This species is now very scarce in Europe, the remaining population being confined to Spain, including Mallorca and south-east Europe, especially Greece. Hunting, poisoning, habitat destruction and improved stock management have all contributed to its decline. It frequents forested and low mountainous areas, choosing a tree or cliff-site for the nest. The nest is a large structure of twigs, branches, grass and other materials. As the sites are used in successive years the nests may become huge (up to 300 cm in diameter). Incubation is shared as is the care of the chick. It is only loosely colonial and is not gregarious like Griffon Vultures. The food is largely carrion, mainly large mammals, though some live prey, such as small mammals and reptiles, may be taken.

The species is not migratory, though some dispersal from the breeding colonies occurs.

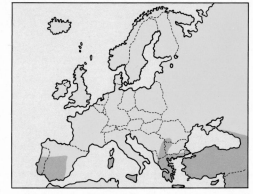

Length:	105 cm
Wing length:	♂ 77 cm, ♀ 80 cm
Weight:	ca 8000 g
Voice:	Hoarse grating calls during breeding, sometimes hissing
Breeding period:	End of February to April, 1 brood per year
Size of clutch:	1 egg
Colour of egg:	White to red-brown, with light or dark rusty patches
Size of egg:	90 × 70 mm
Incubation:	50—55 days
Fledging period:	Nidicolous; able to fly at ca 4 months

Spain (Mey)

Spain (Mey)

Lammergeier (Gypaetus barbatus)

This is Europe's rarest vulture, with under a hundred pairs left. It frequents remote mountainous areas, nesting in caves or on cliff ledges, and usually has several alternative sites. The nest is a massive pile of branches with a lining of wool, hair and dung. Both sexes share incubation, though the ♀ takes the greater part.

It feeds mainly on bones from fresh carcases, dropping the larger bones from a height so that they break on flat rocks. Tortoises are dealt with in a similar manner, though the taking of live prey is not frequent. It does not associate with other vultures at a carcase, waiting till it can feed alone.

It has a spectacular aerial display prior to nesting and the pair-bond is probably for life.

Poisoning has much reduced the European population, and, though it is endangered, the recent decline seems to have slowed up.

The species is mostly resident, with some dispersal from nesting area, though exceptional outside breeding range.

Length:	♂ 110 cm, ♀ 119 cm
Wing length:	♂ 80 cm, ♀ 82 cm
Weight:	♂ 5000 g, ♀ 6900 g
Voice:	Normally silent, though a whistling 'pheee' in display. Young birds: 'wee wee'
Breeding period:	Laying from end of December, 1 brood per year. Replacement clutch known only in captivity
Size of clutch:	1–2 (3) eggs, one chick survives
Colour of eggs:	Light to dark rust-brown, often with little dark brown speckles
Size of eggs:	83 × 65 mm
Incubation:	55–60 days, beginning from first egg
Fledging period:	Nidicolous; able to fly at 110 days

, zoo photograph (Li)

Sub-adult, zoo photograph (Li)

Zoo photograph, Innsbruck, Austria (Li)

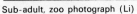

*t) Lammergeier (lower) and Egyptian Vulture ad., Anatolia, Turkey, 1975 (Li)

137

Golden Eagle (Aquila chrysaetos)

The Golden Eagle inhabits mountainous or upland areas and undisturbed forests. Nest-sites are usually on a cliff-ledge or in a tree, and several eyries are used in rotation by a pair. The nest is a large structure of branches, twigs and plant matter, lined with wool or grass. It may reach a massive size (up to 5 m), being built up in successive years. Both sexes take part in nest-building though ♀ does the larger share. This applies to incubation also.

When hunting, the Golden Eagle flies close to the ground, quartering an area. It also uses prominent perching sites and ranges over an extensive area, sometimes attaining a great height on thermals. Prey is very varied, mostly medium-sized mammals such as hares or birds and reptiles. Prey up to size of Chamois, swans and cranes is known. Tortoises are broken open by dropping from a height on to rocks. Some carrion is taken, particularly where live prey species are scarce.

It is predominantly resident, though juveniles disperse up to 200—400 km. The northern population is migratory, moving to southern Scandinavia and occasionally to west European lowlands.

Migration: Late September to December, probably returning in March—April.

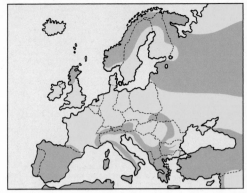

Length:	♂ 80 cm, ♀ 85 cm
Wing length:	♂ 59 cm, ♀ 66 cm
Weight:	♂ 3500 g, ♀ 5000 g
Voice:	'Way-aa' and 'kyk', not very vocal. Fledglings: 'klee-uk'
Breeding period:	Mid-March to May, 1 brood per year. Replacement clutch very rare
Size of clutch:	2 (1–3) eggs
Colour of eggs:	Whitish, with or without brown or muddy patches
Size of eggs:	75 × 59 mm
Incubation:	43–44 days, beginning from first egg
Fledging period:	Nidicolous; flying well at 74–80 days

t eyrie, Anatolia, 1973 (Li)

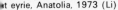

d. ♀ at eyrie with juv., Anatolia, Turkey, 31.5.1973 (Li)

Golden Eagle mobbed by Kestrel, Anatolia, 1973 (Li)

Anatolia, 27.5.1975 (Li)

Imperial Eagle (Aquila heliaca)

The Imperial Eagle is an inhabitant of lowland steppes, open woodland and wetlands. It takes a variety of prey, mainly small to medium-sized mammals, some birds, carrion and reptiles.

The nests are sited in trees; rarely in low bushes or on cliffs. Both sexes take part in nest-building, constructing a large base of branches and twigs, lined with grass, fur and refuse. Fresh green vegetation is placed on the nest during breeding.

Two populations occur in Europe. The Spanish race *adalberti* is severely endangered and is down to *ca* 50 pairs. The eastern European race is more numerous, though this, too, has suffered a decline due to habitat destruction, pesticide residues and poisoning.

The Spanish race is largely resident; eastern birds are partially migratory, young birds moving furthest. They winter in Africa, parts of the Middle East and south-east Europe.

Migration: Autumn passage September—October, return in February— April, migration not fully known.

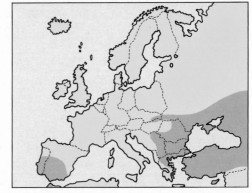

Length:	80 cm
Wing length:	♂ 57 cm, ♀ 60 cm (*heliaca*)
Weight:	3000 g
Voice:	'Tyah', 'owk, owk', deeper than Golden Eagle
Breeding period:	End of March, April, 1 brood per year. Replacement clutch possible
Size of clutch:	2–3 (1) eggs
Colour of eggs:	Whitish with a few grey or brown patches
Size of eggs:	73 × 56 mm
Incubation:	43 days, beginning from first egg
Fledging period:	Nidicolous; able to fly at 65–70 days

rn race (*A. h. heliaca*), 4.7.1944 (Mey)

Spanish race (*Aquila heliaca adalberti*) (Mey)

Juv. at eyrie with prey (ground-squirrel), Anatolia, Turkey, 11.6.1973 (Li)

Young, a few days old, Anatolia, 6.5.1975 (Li)

141

Lesser Spotted Eagle

(Aquila pomarina)

The Lesser Spotted Eagle breeds mainly in eastern Europe, frequenting wooded country with marshy areas. In the breeding areas it feeds mainly on small mammals, birds and reptiles as well as some insects.

The nest is built of branches and twigs, lined with green vegetation, and is sited in a tree, not at the top but at a fork. The species is very territorial and returns to the same site each year.

The second chick to hatch almost invariably dies as a result of aggression from the elder chick.

Lesser Spotted Eagles are wholly migratory, wintering mainly in eastern Africa south of the Sahara. The migratory route is principally through the Bosphorus and Levant countries, leaving via Suez on the return passage.

Migration: Dispersal from mid-August with main movements in late September to November, returning in March and April.

The larger Spotted Eagle (*Aquila clanga*) has a more easterly breeding distribution and favours wetter habitats. It winters in Southern Europe, Turkey and the Middle East as well as Africa.

Length:	61—66 cm
Wing length:	♂ 46 cm, ♀ 48 cm
Weight:	1500 g
Voice:	Long-drawn whistles, 'weeeeck' or a barking, 'chuck, chuck'
Breeding period:	End of April, May, 1 brood per year. Replacement clutch unknown
Size of clutch:	2 (1—3) eggs
Colour of eggs:	White, with variable red-brown patches
Size of eggs:	63 × 51 mm
Incubation:	38—40 days, beginning from first egg
Fledging period:	Nidicolous; able to fly at *ca* 7 weeks

with almost fledged young (Mey)

Ad. with four-week-old young, East Slovakia, July 1968 (Mey)

Juveniles at rest (Mey)

East Slovakia (Mey)

Booted Eagle (Hieraetus pennatus)

The Booted Eagle is found in forest areas with some heath or scrub. It ranges over a wide variety of habitats in hunting, often using thermals to attain height. It feeds mostly on small to medium-sized birds, small mammals and reptiles. It has a prominent aerial display, often performed over the nest site. The nest is usually built in a tree, though cliff sites may be used. Often an old nest of another raptor serves as the foundation. The nest is constructed of branches and twigs lined with leaves.

The species is migratory, exceptionally wintering in the Mediterranean countries. It favours short sea-crossings using Gibraltar, the Bosphorus and the Sicilian Channel. It winters over a wide area of Africa south of the Sahara.

Migration: Dispersal from late August with main movements in late September to October. Spring passage from February, though mainly late March and April.

The Bonelli's Eagle (*Hieraetus fasciatus*) is found in rocky, mountainous country in southern Europe. It is largely resident, though will disperse to lowland habitats in winter.

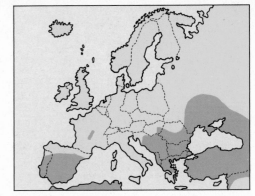

Length:	52 cm
Wing length:	♂ 36 cm, ♀ 39 cm
Weight:	♂ 716 g, ♀ 960 g
Voice:	'Kee kee kee', also trilling and cackling noises
Breeding period:	May, June, 1 brood per year
Size of clutch:	2 (1–3) eggs
Colour of eggs:	White with a few light brown patches. As brooding progresses they darken as a result of green material in the nest
Size of eggs:	54 × 44 mm
Incubation:	35–38 days
Fledging period:	Nidicolous; able to fly at 50–54 days

♂, light phase, bringing nest-material, 14.6.1976 (Li)

Ad. ♀, light phase, at eyrie, Greece, 11.6.1976 (Li)

Light phase, Anatolia, Turkey, 1973 (Li)

Greece, 11.6.1976 (Li)

145

Buzzard (Buteo buteo)

The Buzzard is the commonest and most widespread large raptor in Europe. It favours open habitats with some woodland or forest and uplands or low mountainous country. The eyrie is invariably sited in a tree, though cliff-sites may be used and even ground-sites. Each pair has a large number of alternative eyries used in rotation. The nest is built by both sexes and is constructed of branches and twigs lined with green foliage. Both sexes share in incubation.

Buzzards take a wide variety of prey, mostly small mammals, birds, reptiles and amphibians, large insects and carrion. The diversity of prey enables the species to feed in many habitats.

The species is resident, dispersive or totally migratory, depending on population. Birds from north and east of the range are the most migratory, large numbers leaving Europe via the Bosphorus or eastern Black Sea to winter in Africa and parts of the Middle East. Northern birds tend to move south-west through Europe as far as Spain. British birds are largely resident.

Migration: Dispersal from August with main passage in September—October. Spring movement in March and early April.

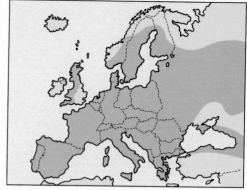

Length:	♂ 53 cm, ♀ 56 cm
Wing length:	♂ 38 cm, ♀ 40 cm
Weight:	♂ 800 g, ♀ 900 g
Voice:	Long drawn-out mewing, 'hee-ow'
Breeding period:	April to June, 1 brood per year. Replacement clutch possible
Size of clutch:	2–4 (1–5) eggs
Colour of eggs:	White, with more or less numerous yellow-brown or red-brown blotches
Size of eggs:	55 × 45 mm
Incubation:	33–34 days, beginning from second egg
Fledging period:	Nidicolous; able to fly at 50–55 days

ia, 14.5.1975 (Pf)

Ad. ♀ on eyrie, Bavaria, West Germany, 1965 (Li)

Nestlings, 27 days old, Bavaria, 8.6.1975 (Pf)

Baden-Württemberg, West Germany, 1974 (Li)

Rough-legged Buzzard

(Buteo lagopus)

The Rough-legged Buzzard is a bird of the open northern tundra. It rarely occurs in wooded areas, preferring broad, open country with rocky outcrops. They feed principally on small mammals, particularly voles and lemmings, and the cyclical variation in the populations of these prey species has a marked effect on the breeding biology. In good rodent years the species will inhabit a wider area, lay more eggs and produce a higher number of chicks. The nest-site is on the ground or on a rocky outcrop, and may be used in successive years. It is a small structure of twigs and other vegetation built by both sexes. The ♂ takes only a small part, if any, in incubation, though both parents care for the chicks.
The Rough-legged Buzzard is wholly migratory, moving south to winter from southern Sweden and the east coast of Britain through eastern Europe. When food is scarce or during hard weather the birds may move further south and west, even to the Mediterranean.

Migration: Dependent to some extent on availability of food, but may disperse from August, mostly October–November with return in late March and April.

Length:	60 cm
Wing length:	♂ 42 cm, ♀ 44 cm
Weight:	1000 g
Voice:	Similar to Buzzard, 'pee-you'
Breeding period:	Mid-May, June, 1 brood per year. Probable replacement clutch
Size of clutch:	3–5 (2–7) eggs
Colour of eggs:	Greenish to dirty white, with red-brown to dark brown patches
Size of eggs:	55 × 43 mm
Incubation:	28–31 days
Fledging period:	Nidicolous; young leave eyrie at 39–43 days

tland, Sweden, June 1974 (Pa)

) Rough-legged Buzzard at eyrie, Handöl, Sweden (Wö)

Ground-nest in the tundra of Finnish Lappland, June 1970 (Willy)

149

Long-legged Buzzard

(Buteo rufinus)

The Long-legged Buzzard is found in low-lying arid areas, including semi-desert and steppes. It favours open country, where it feeds on small mammals, reptiles and large insects, either quartering the ground in low circling flight or pouncing from a prominent perch. The nest-site is usually on a crag or cliff-ledge, though occasionally on the ground or in a tree. The nest is constructed from branches and twigs, lined with grass, wool or other soft material.

The European population is migratory, wintering in Turkey and the Middle East down into Africa. The migratory routes are not fully understood, as numbers seen at main raptor migration watchpoints are very small.

Migration: Timing not well known but recorded from August—October with return from February—April.

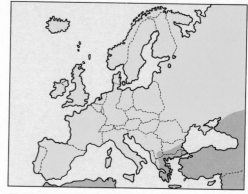

Length:	♂ 55 cm, ♀ 65 cm
Wing length:	♂ 44 cm, ♀ 46 cm
Weight:	♂ 1150 g, ♀ 1300 g
Voice:	Cf. Buzzard, but higher, 'aaa-ah'
Breeding period:	March to May, 1 brood per year. Replacement clutch probable
Size of clutch:	3–4 (2–5) eggs
Colour of eggs:	White with sparse brown patches
Size of eggs:	60 × 47 mm
Incubation:	28 days
Fledging period:	Nidicolous; able to fly at ca 41 days

...olia, Turkey, 28.5.1974 (Li)

Ad. ♀ at eyrie with prey, Macedonia, Yugoslavia, 1971 (Li)

Anatolia, 23.5.1974 (Li)

Anatolia, 28.5.1974 (Li)

151

Sparrowhawk (Accipiter nisus)

The Sparrowhawk is found in wooded country of all types, though prefers conifers for nesting. It hunts by surprise, flying low and keeping near cover. It feeds almost entirely on small birds; due to the large size difference between sexes the ♀ is able to take much larger prey species than the ♂.

The nest site is in the fork of a tree, close to the trunk. It is a loose pile of twigs, often founded on an old nest of Woodpigeon (*Columba aplumbus*). The ♂ does most of the nest-building whilst the ♀ broods and rears the young alone.

The species has declined over much of its range due to the use of organochlorine pesticides, but there is now signs of a recovery.

The species is wholly migratory in the north of its range, birds from Fenno-Scandia and the USSR moving to southern Europe, North Africa and the Middle East in winter. Continental birds tend to migrate south-west to Iberia and British birds are largely resident.

Migration: Main autumn movements mid-September to November, returning in March and April.

Length:	♂ 28 cm, ♀ 38 cm
Wing length:	♂ 20 cm, ♀ 24 cm
Weight:	♂ 140 g, ♀ 250 g
Voice:	'Kek-kek-kek', ♀ significantly higher; usually heard near nest
Breeding period:	End of April to June, 1 brood per year. Replacement clutch frequent
Size of clutch:	4–6 (3–7) eggs
Colour of eggs:	White with more or less numerous patches of violet-grey or chestnut brown
Size of eggs:	39 × 31 mm
Incubation:	33–36 days, beg. from fourth or last egg
Fledging period:	Nidicolous; able to fly at *ca* 30 days. ♂♂ develop faster than ♀♀ chicks

♀ feeding young, Bavaria, 1959 (Li)

15-day-old nestlings, Bavaria, 5.6.1976 (Pf)

Bavaria, 1959 (Li)

♂ (behind) bringing prey to nest, Bavaria, West Germany, 10.5.1971 (Pf)

153

Levant Sparrowhawk

(Accipiter brevipes)

The Levant Sparrowhawk is found in lowland deciduous forests, and some upland areas in south-east Europe. It feeds mainly on lizards and large insects, hunting from moderate heights and stooping on to prey, unlike other Accipiters.

The nest is sited in a deciduous tree and is a small structure of twigs lined with green foliage; sometimes old nests of Hooded Crow are used. Nest-building, incubation and care of young is done by the ♀, though the ♂ brings food to the nest.

The species is wholly migratory and is very gregarious when on passage and sometimes in winter quarters. European birds move out through the Bosphorus and more eastern birds use the eastern Black Sea route. It winters in Africa, though its exact range is unknown.

Migration: Autumn passage mid-August to October, mainly September, returning in March and April.

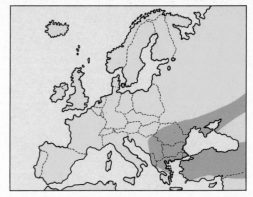

Length:	♂ 33 cm, ♀ 38 cm
Wing length:	♂ 22 cm, ♀ 23.5 cm
Weight:	♂ 160 g, ♀ 230 g
Voice:	At eyrie 'awick awick awick' in rapid series
Breeding period:	Mid-May, June–July, 1 brood per year. Replacement clutch possible
Size of clutch:	3–5 eggs
Colour of eggs:	White with a green sheen. During brooding, become patched with brown through disturbance of the nest-lining
Size of eggs:	40 × 31 mm
Incubation:	30–35 days, starting with 1st or 2nd egg
Fledging period:	Nidicolous; remaining 40–45 days in nest

a pause in brooding, Greece, 29.5.1978 (Li)

Ad. ♂ at nest, Greece, 29.5.1978 (Li)

Nestlings, Greece, 6.7.1977 (Li)

Greece, 23.5.1978 (Li)

Goshawk (Accipiter gentilis)

The Goshawk is essentially a forest bird, preferring conifers to deciduous woodland. It will inhabit mountainous areas up to the treeline. The European population has suffered a decline due to human persecution and also the use of pesticides. In some areas it is now increasing, helped by afforestation and by release of falconers' birds.

It feeds on large birds and mammals up to the size of a hare. The diet depends on availability of prey species in the area and important species are pigeons, grouse, crows and thrushes. The nest is a large structure of branches and twigs sited in the fork of a tree; some nests are used in successive years. Incubation is mainly by the ♀ and she takes care of rearing the young, though the ♂ brings food items to nest.

It is not as migratory as other European Accipiters, but there is considerable dispersal away from breeding areas. Northern birds move the furthest, some to south-west Europe, and the species has been recorded in small numbers at Gibraltar and the Bosphorus.

Migration: Dispersal from August with main movements in late September to November, return in March and April.

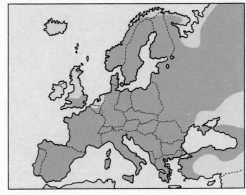

Length:	♂ 50 cm, ♀ 60 cm
Wing length:	♂ 31 cm, ♀ 35 cm
Weight:	♂ 860 g, ♀ 1300 g
Voice:	'Kekekekeke', louder and deeper than Sparrowhawk
Breeding period:	April–June, 1 brood per year. Replacement clutch possible
Size of clutch:	3–4 (2–6) eggs
Colour of eggs:	Greenish white
Size of eggs:	60 × 46 mm
Incubation:	35–38 days, beg. before clutch complete
Fledging period:	Nidicolous; young leave eyrie after 40 days, ♂♂ earlier

♀ at eyrie, Bavaria, 1962 (Rei)

Nestlings, 37 days old, 27.6.1975 (Pf)

Bavaria, 1965 (Li)

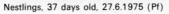

Ad. ♂ taking off, Bavaria, West Germany, 1960 (Li)

Red Kite (Milvus milvus)

The Red Kite frequents rugged landscapes with deciduous woodland or forest. It feeds on a great variety of prey including small mammals, birds, fish, insects, reptiles and carrion. It is an effortless flier and hunts by soaring, often to considerable heights to locate food.

The nest is sited on a main fork in a tree and is constructed of twigs with a lining that includes grass, wool, rags, paper and other refuse. Old nests of Buzzard and Raven may be used. The nest-building is done mainly by the ♀ with materials supplied by the ♂. The ♀ does most of the incubating and both sexes share in the care of the young.

The species declined in numbers and range throughout most of Europe, but this decline is now halted in some areas due to protection. There is a relict Welsh population of about thirty pairs.

Outside the breeding season Red Kites will form small flocks where food is plentiful. The eastern and central European populations are largely migratory, moving to Iberia, North Africa, south-east Europe and the Middle East. Other populations are largely resident.

Migration: Dispersal from August with main passage September—October. Spring movements from late February to April.

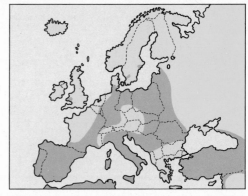

Length:	♂ 62 cm, ♀ 64 cm
Wing length:	♂ 49 cm, ♀ 50 cm
Weight:	♂ 950 g, ♀ 1050 g
Voice:	Like Black Kite, 'whee-wheehee-wheehee'
Breeding period:	April, May, 1 brood per year.. Replacement clutch possible
Size of clutch:	2—3 (1—5) eggs
Colour of eggs:	Whitish with more or less numerous light brown patches
Size of eggs:	57 × 46 mm
Incubation:	32 days, beginning from first egg
Fledging period:	Nidicolous; able to fly at 48—50 days

...ria, 19.5.1977 (Pf)

Bavaria, West Germany, 1979 (Ka)

Nestlings, 10 days old, Bavaria, 16.5.1975 (Pf)

Bavaria, 23.5.1975 (Pf)

Black Kite (Milvus migrans)

The Black Kite frequents lowland areas with woodland, particularly near water. It is also found near human habitation scavenging on rubbish tips and can be found in some cities, e.g. Istanbul. It is an opportunist feeder, taking much carrion and scavenging on refuse. It will also rob other birds of food and take a variety of live food, particularly fish, small mammals, birds, reptiles and insects.

It usually nests in trees, though cliff-sites and old buildings may be used. The nest is built mainly by the ♂ from twigs and small branches with much refuse in the form of paper, rags, wool or hair and sometimes green foliage. Incubation is largely by ♀, food being brought by ♂ who also provisions ♀ during rearing of young.

The European population is fairly stable, with decreases in some areas but an increase in others.

The species is wholly migratory, a very few wintering in Mediterranean countries. Most cross into Africa via Gibraltar, with smaller numbers using the Bosphorus, and eastern birds passing round the east end of the Black Sea. The main wintering areas are in West Africa.

Migration: First departures in July with bulk in August to September, return from late February to April.

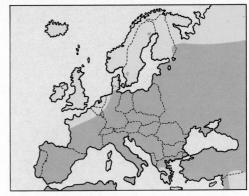

Length:	57 cm
Wing length:	45 cm
Weight:	850 g
Voice:	Trilling 'wirhihihihi'
Breeding period:	Mid-April, May, 1 brood per year. Replacement clutch rare
Size of clutch:	2–3 (1–5) eggs
Colour of eggs:	Whitish with (usually) few fine light brown patches
Size of eggs:	54 × 42 mm
Incubation:	28–30 days, beg. from 1st or 2nd egg
Fledging period:	Nidicolous; able to fly at 42–45 days

k Kite at twilight, Turkey, 31.5.1966 (Fe)

) Imm., Bavaria, West Germany, 1970 (Li)

Anatolia, Turkey, 1974 (Li)

Greece, 15.5.1972 (Li)

White-tailed Eagle

(Haliaeetus albicilla)

The White-tailed Eagle inhabits wild, wooded country near inland waters over much of its range. In the north, however, it frequents sea-cliffs, islands and tundra.

It takes a wide variety of food, particularly fish, though mammals, birds and reptiles are also taken. It scavenges on carrion and will also rob other birds of food.

The nest is a huge structure of branches, twigs and other plant materials. It is usually sited in a tree, though in northern Europe cliff-ledges are commonly used. Pairs may have many alternative eyries and these are used in successive or alternate years. Both sexes take part in nest-building, incubation and care of the young, though ♀ takes larger share. The population was much reduced due to human persecution and use of toxic pesticides. There has been some recovery due to increased protection, though poisoning of adults still occurs.

In Europe, adult birds are resident throughout the year except in certain areas where prey is absent in winter. Young birds move away from natal areas, most moving south or south-west.

Migration: Dispersal from September with main movements in October–November, returning in March and April.

Length:	♂ 70 cm, ♀ 90 cm
Wing length:	♂ 60 cm, ♀ 66 cm
Weight:	♂ 4100 g, ♀ 5500 g
Voice:	'Klee-klee-kee', 'klick', and 'kok'
Breeding period:	February, March, April, 1 brood per year. Replacement clutch rare
Size of clutch:	2 (1–4) eggs
Colour of eggs:	White, rarely with a few light brown patches
Size of eggs:	75 × 58 mm
Incubation:	38–42 days, beginning from first egg
Fledging period:	Nidicolous; able to fly at ca 75 days

1., Rundø, Norway, 1974 (Mo)

Imm. with carrion, Sweden (Ar)

Schleswig-Holstein, West Germany, 1.4.1960 (Wa)

*) ♀ at eyrie, photographed in a reserve, 1979 (Ka)

163

Honey Buzzard (Pernis apivorus)

The Honey Buzzard is a bird of deciduous woodland, though not averse to conifers if feeding conditions are suitable. It feeds on the larvae of wasps and bees and is able to dig out their nests, protected from the stings of the adult insects by the scale-like feathers of the head. It will also take other insects, small mammals, reptiles and young birds.

It nests on a branch or in a fork of a large tree, particularly Beech. The nest is built of twigs, often almost entirely fresh growth with green leaves, and further sprigs of foliage are added through the breeding season. Old nests of Crows or Buzzard may be used at times. Both sexes share in nest-building, incubation and care of the young, the ♀ taking the larger share.

The species is entirely migratory, wintering in Africa south of the Sahara. Large numbers of migrating birds congregate at short sea-crossings such as Falsterbo, the Bosphorus and Gibraltar, others using the eastern Black Sea route.

Migration: Late August to November, returning in April to early June.

Length:	55 cm
Wing length:	41 cm
Weight:	800 g
Voice:	A mournful 'pee-hah' or a clucking 'gagagag' at eyrie
Breeding period:	End of May to July, 1 brood per year. Replacement clutch possible but rare
Size of clutch:	2 (1–3) eggs
Colour of eggs:	Whitish, with layers of red-brown spotting and clouding
Size of eggs:	52 × 41 mm
Incubation:	30–35 days, beginning from first egg
Fledging period:	Nidicolous; able to fly at 40–44 days

freshly lined eyrie, Bavaria, 30.7.1972 (Li)

Kühkopf, Hessen, West Germany, 1.6.1963 (Pf)

Bavaria, 25.6.1965 (Pf)

Ad. ♂ at eyrie with nestlings, Bavaria, West Germany, 22.7.1972 (Li)

165

Marsh Harrier (Circus aeruginosus)

The Marsh Harrier frequents wetland areas especially with large reedbeds or other emergent vegetation. It hunts over reeds or open country, quartering the ground in low flight. It feeds on a variety of small mammals and birds including nestlings. It is solitary or loosely colonial, and several pairs may breed in extensive reedbeds. The nest is a large pile of reeds, grasses and twigs built by the ♀. The ♀ also incubates alone and cares for the young, though the ♂ brings food which he passes to the ♀ in flight. The ♂ rarely visits the nest. There is a striking aerial display involving food-passes by the ♂, the ♀ flipping on to her back in flight to receive the prey.

A few birds are resident in their breeding areas, including British birds. The majority, however, migrate. Some winter in Mediterranean countries but most move to Africa south of the Sahara. Mediterranean crossings are probably on a broad front as the species does not concentrate at raptor watchpoints like Bosphorus or Gibraltar.

Migration: Dispersal from August with main movements in September—October. Return passage in March and April.

Length:	48–56 cm
Wing length:	♂ 39 cm, ♀ 41 cm
Weight:	600 g
Voice:	Whistling 'klee-ah, cuik, pee-ah' or 'kekekek'
Breeding period:	April, May, June, 1 brood per year. Replacement clutch possible
Size of clutch:	3–8 (2–10) eggs
Colour of eggs:	Whitish
Size of eggs:	50 × 38 mm
Incubation:	30–38 days, beginning from first egg
Fledging period:	Nidicolous; able to fly at 40 days; may leave nest to scatter in surrounding area at 30 days

nest with young, Föhr, W. Germany, June 1967 (Qu)

Imm. about to bathe, Yugoslavia, 1974 (Li)

Ad. ♀, Föhr, June 1975 (Qu)

Nest with young birds, Greece, 16.6.1976 (Li)

167

Hen Harrier (Circus cyaneus)

The Hen Harrier is found in a variety of habitats including heath and moorland, forest clearings, margins of wetlands, plantations of young trees and low scrub. It hunts in typical harrier fashion by quartering the ground in low flight, dropping to pounce on prey. Food is mainly small mammals and birds including nestlings. Songbirds such as Meadow Pipit form a large part of the diet.

The nest is sited on the ground, usually in low cover. It is built mainly by the ♀ of grass, heather and similar plant matter. The ♀ incubates alone and the ♂♂ may be polygamous in some areas. The ♀ feeds the young with food brought by the ♂ at first; later both parents hunt. There is a spectacular aerial display involving food-passes.

Outside the breeding season the species may roost colonially with up to thirty birds at one site.

The species is not highly migratory; birds from the north and eastern parts of the range move to winter in western Europe, a few moving as far as North Africa and the Middle East. Birds breeding in central Europe are less migratory, though there is some dispersal away from breeding areas. Often found wintering on agricultural land, downland and marshes.

Migration: Dispersal from late August, main movements in late September to November, returning in March and April.

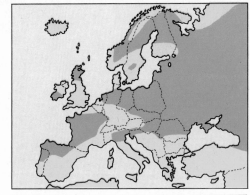

Length:	♂ 43 cm, ♀ 51 cm
Wing length:	♂ 34 cm, ♀ 37 cm
Weight:	♂ 430 g, ♀ 470 g
Voice:	'Kekekeke, kiriwikik, jee-ooo'
Breeding period:	Mid-April to June, 1 brood per year. Replacement clutch possible
Size of clutch:	4–6 (3) eggs
Colour of eggs:	Whitish, sometimes with brown patches
Size of eggs:	45 × 35 mm
Incubation:	29–30 days, from 2nd, 3rd or 4th egg
Fledging period:	Nidicolous; able to fly at 35 days, ♂♂ earlier than ♀♀

Nestling, Amrum, June 1967 (Qu)

Amrum, May 1967 (Qu)

♂, Amrum, Schleswig-Holstein, West Germany, e 1967 (Qu)
♀ at nest, central Norway, 12.7.1967 (Sy)

169

Montagu's Harrier (Circus pygargus)

The Montagu's Harrier is found in habitats varying from farmland to wetland margins and heathland with scrub growth. It prefers taller vegetation for nesting than the Hen Harrier and requires undisturbed country. It feeds on small birds and rodents, hunting by flying low over the ground, often following lines of vegetation. The nest site is on the ground in tall vegetation, reeds, heather, young trees and even in cornfields. The species may nest in loose colonies and some ♂♂ are bigamous. The nest is a shallow mound of reeds, twigs and grass, built by the ♀. The ♀ incubates alone being fed by the ♂ who also brings food for the nestlings. There is a spectacular aerial display involving food-passes from ♂ to ♀.

The species has suffered a considerable decline in many areas mainly due to habitat changes. It is now extremely rare in Britain.

The Montagu's Harrier is wholly migratory. It is not averse to broad sea-crossings but large numbers use the Gibraltar crossing on their way to winter in tropical Africa.

Migration: Dispersal from late July, main movements in late August to October, returning in March–May.

Length:	41–46 cm
Wing length:	37 cm
Weight:	300 g
Voice:	'Kekek', 'chuk-chuk', 'psee'
Breeding period:	Beginning of May, June, 1 brood per year. Replacement clutch possible in July
Size of clutch:	3–5 (2–10) eggs
Colour of eggs:	Smooth, white
Size of eggs:	41 × 33 mm
Incubation:	28–30 days, beginning from first egg
Fledging period:	Nidicolous; able to fly at 35–40 days

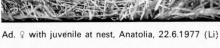

rtship flight: ♀ below, ♂ above, Anatolia, Turkey, .1975 (Li)
) Ad. ♂ at feeding place (Li)

Ad. ♀ with juvenile at nest, Anatolia, 22.6.1977 (Li)

Anatolia, 22.6.1977 (Li)

171

Short-toed Eagle (Circaetus gallicus)

The Short-toed Eagle frequents open country in both lowland and mountainous areas, often near woods or crags which offer suitable nesting sites. A dry climate is necessary for its main food (snakes and lizards) though in the north of its range it uses wetter habitat where grass-snakes are plentiful. It normally builds its nest in a low tree, though cliff-ledges may be used, or nests of other birds. The ♂ brings most of the twigs, sticks and greenery with the ♀ building the nest. Both sexes will incubate, but mainly the ♀. It is also the ♀ who feeds the young, though often using food brought by the ♂.

The species is strongly territorial, the ♂ driving intruders away. In courtship display the ♂ often carries a snake or other prey in its bill. This is sometimes given to the ♀ in flight.

Short-toed Eagles are migratory, wintering in a belt across Africa south of the Sahara. It favours short sea-crossings and congregates at narrows, especially Gibraltar.

Migration: Dispersal from August-with main passage in September to mid-October. Return passage in March and April.

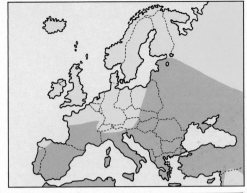

Length:	♂ 65 cm, ♀ 68 cm
Wing length:	♂ 52 cm, ♀ 54 cm
Weight:	♂ 1750 g, ♀ 1860 g
Voice:	'Klee-oh' or 'klee-yah', and mewing sounds
Breeding period:	May–July, 1 brood per year. Replacement clutch possible
Size of clutch:	Invariably 1 egg
Colour of egg:	White
Size of egg:	73 × 58 mm
Incubation:	45–47 days
Fledging period:	Nidicolous; able to fly at ca 73 days

tolia, 25.6.1977 (Li)

♀ with young at eyrie, 27.6.1977 (Li)

Anatolia, 1972 (Wa)

) ♂ with lizard, Anatolia, Turkey, 25.6.1977 (Li)

173

Osprey (Pandion haliaetus)

The Osprey lives almost exclusively on fish and is restricted to inland and coastal waters. In the north of its range it is a tree-nester and may breed some km from the nearest lake or river. In the south it will nest on cliff-sites and rocky islets on the coast. The nest is a large structure of branches and twigs often lined with grass or heather. Both sexes share in nest-building, the ♂ taking the larger share. In incubation the ♀ takes the major role and the ♂ brings most food for the young. Food is obtained by a spectacular plunge-dive and carried in the talons to a perch where it is devoured.

The species suffered a marked decline in population mainly due to human persecution for fishery interests. More recently, disturbance, pollution and possibly pesticides have contributed to further contraction of range. Re-colonisation of Scotland from the late 1950s is the only sign of increase. The species is mainly a summer visitor to Europe, though some winter in the Mediterranean. Most birds move to West Africa. Not requiring short-sea crossings, they migrate on a broad front.

Migration: Main autumn movements in September and October with return in late March and April.

Length:	55–58 cm
Wing length:	♂ 46 cm, ♀ 49 cm
Weight:	1500 g
Voice:	'Cheep-cheep-cheep-chirp-chirp-chirp', falling in pitch
Breeding period:	April to early June, 1 brood per year. Replacement clutch possible in the south
Size of clutch:	2–3 (1–4) eggs
Colour of eggs:	Whitish, with red-brown patches
Size of eggs:	60 × 45 mm
Incubation:	35–38 days, from first or second egg
Fledging period:	Nidicolous; able to fly at 53–59 days

leswig-Holstein, West Germany (Ki)

") Ad., Sweden (Ar)

Almost fledged young, Sweden (Ar)

Sweden (Ar)

175

Hobby (Falco subbuteo)

The Hobby is found in a wide variety of habitats throughout most of Europe. It nests in trees using the old nests of other birds, particularly crows or other birds of prey, and does no nest-building of its own. The ♀ incubates alone and the ♂ supplies most of the food which is fed to the young by the ♀. The Hobby is an agile, swift flier and captures its prey in flight. Small birds and insects make up the bulk of the diet, insects being eaten on the wing whilst held in the talons. Some small mammals, reptiles and terrestrial insects are also taken. It is often active in the evening, working roosts of hirundines and, occasionally, bats.

The European population has declined in some areas but in others, including Britain, it is fairly stable.

It is a summer visitor to Europe, winter records being exceptional. Most of the population winters in the southern part of Africa. It does not congregate at raptor watchpoints and probably makes broad-front crossings of the Mediterranean.

Migration: Mainly mid-September to mid-November with return in April and May.

Length:	♂ 33 cm, ♀ 34 cm
Wing length:	♂ 25 cm, ♀ 27 cm
Weight:	♂ 200 g, ♀ 250 g
Voice:	'Tyutyu, tyu', like Wryneck, 'ghee-ghee-ghee'
Breeding period:	End of May to July, 1 brood per year. Replacement clutch possible
Size of clutch:	2–4, usually 3 eggs
Colour of eggs:	Yellowish white with red-brown and yellow patches
Size of eggs:	43 × 32 mm
Incubation:	*ca* 28 days, beginning from second egg
Fledging period:	Nidicolous; able to fly at 28–34 days

...tolia, Turkey, 1977 (Li)

♀ bringing prey to eyrie, Baden-Württemberg, 1961 (Li)

Baden-Württemberg, 1961 (Li)

♀ at eyrie with young, Baden-Württemberg, West Germany, 1961 (Li)

Peregrine (Falco peregrinus)

The Peregrine is now an extremely rare bird throughout most of Europe, the reason for its drastic decline being the use of organochloride pesticides which have caused heavy adult mortality as well as reduced breeding success. It is now subject to strict protection in many countries and there are signs of a halt to the decrease in some areas, particularly Britain, which is now its European stronghold.

It breeds on cliff-ledges, crags and occasionally on old buildings. It makes no nest, the eggs being laid in a scrape in soft earth; it will also use the remains of old nests of other birds. Incubation is mainly by the ♀, the ♂ hunting and bringing food to the nest. It feeds mainly on birds, usually taken on the wing after a dramatic stoop. Pigeons, seabirds, wildfowl and Starlings are important prey items, though it will take birds from the size of Goldcrest to Heron.

Birds from the northern part of the range move south or south-west in winter. British birds are largely resident.

Migration: August—November, return in March—May (northern populations).

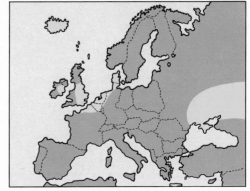

Length:	♂ 40 cm, ♀ 48 cm
Wing length:	♂ 30 cm, ♀ 35 cm
Weight:	♂ 600 g, ♀ 900 g
Voice:	Series of calls like 'cak-cak-cak', also a sharp 'kee-aca'
Breeding period:	April—June, 1 brood per year. Replacement clutch possible
Size of clutch:	3–4 (2–6) eggs
Colour of eggs:	Yellowish, with thick red-brown patches
Size of eggs:	51 × 40 mm
Incubation:	29–32 days, from last or penultimate egg
Fledging period:	Nidicolous; able to fly at 36–40 days

klenburg, West Germany. After SW photograph, (Ka)
♀ Falconer's bird (Li)

Young, Bavaria, West Germany, 1972 (Sch)

Mecklenburg. After SW photograph, 1949 (Ka)

179

Saker Falcon (Falco cherrug)

The Saker Falcon is an inhabitant of steppe country, open plains and foothills of mountains. It is often found near wetlands or rivers and also occurs in forests.

It takes a variety of prey, mostly small mammals such as susliks, birds, reptiles and occasionally insects. It hunts by stooping on birds from a height, or low flight, to surprise terrestrial prey.

The nest is on a cliff-ledge or in a tree. No nest material is used so the nest is often in an old nest of another species. Incubation is by both sexes, though the ♀ takes a larger share. Both parents hunt to obtain food for the young, though the ♂ does this at first.

It is a scarce breeding bird in eastern Europe with some decline in population in recent years.

The species is only partially migratory in Europe, though eastern populations are wholly migratory, wintering in the Middle East, Africa and south-east Europe.

Migration: Mainly mid-September to early November, with return in March and April.

Length:	♂ 46 cm, ♀ 52 cm
Wing length:	♂ 36 cm, ♀ 39 cm
Weight:	♂ 800 g, ♀ 1100 g
Voice:	Hoarse series of calls: 'kyak-kyak-kyak'
Breeding period:	April, May, 1 brood per year. Replacement clutch possible
Size of clutch:	3–5 (2–6) eggs
Colour of eggs:	Whitish yellow with fine light brown or reddish brown patches
Size of eggs:	53 × 41 mm
Incubation:	28–30 days, beginning from first egg
Fledging period:	Nidicolous; able to fly at 40–45 days

, Anatolia, 24.6.1977 (Li)

Young bird in cliff eyrie, Anatolia, 12.5.1975 (Li)

Clutch in old Grey Heron's nest, Austria, 1961 (Wa)

') ♀ at eyrie with young, Anatolia, Turkey, 13.5.1975 (Li)

Eleonora's Falcon (Falco eleonorae)

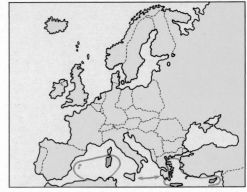

This highly specialised, colonial falcon is found almost entirely on Mediterranean islands, and the world population is under 5000 pairs. It nests on cliff-ledges, on steep slopes and in caves, invariably close to the sea. Colonies are usually 5–50 nests, often close together. No nest is built but old nests of other species are used, or a scrape in bare earth. Incubation is mainly by the ♀ and the ♂ brings most of the food for the young. The species breeds very late in the summer, so that hatching coincides with the autumn passage of passerine birds. It hunts mainly in the early mornings and evenings, taking large insects and a variety of migrant birds, mostly up to size of the Hoopoe (*Upupa epops*). The prey is caught on the wing and held in the talons; insects are often eaten in flight.

The species is wholly migratory, wintering in Madagascar and parts of East Africa. Birds from the entire range move eastwards to the Red Sea in autumn, then southwards.

Migration: October to early November returning in late April to early June.

Length:	♂ 37 cm, ♀ 38 cm
Wing length:	♂ 31 cm, ♀ 32 cm
Weight:	♂ 350 g, ♀ 400 g
Voice:	Three- or four-syllable cries: 'kyek kyek kyek kyek', 'cree cree cree'
Breeding period:	End of July, August, 1 brood per year
Size of clutch:	2–3 (1–4) eggs
Colour of eggs:	White to reddish with cloudy red-brown patches
Size of eggs:	43 × 34 mm
Incubation:	28 days, from first or second egg
Fledging period:	Nidicolous; able to fly at 35–40 days

phase, ♂ left, ♀ right, Greece, 1974 (Li)

Ad. ♀, light phase, Greece, 7.9.1975 (Pf)

Greece, 30.8.1975 (Pf)

Greece, 7.9.1975 (Pf)

183

Lesser Kestrel (Falco naumanni)

The Lesser Kestrel is primarily a bird of warm, lowland areas including steppe, semi-desert and open wooded country. It is a gregarious bird, usually feeding in flocks and breeding in colonies. It feeds mainly on insects taken both on the wing and on the ground. Small mammals, reptiles and nestling birds are also taken at times.

The nests are usually sited on tall buildings, old walls or cliff-ledges. No nesting material is used, the ♀ does most of the incubating and both parents share in rearing the young.

There has been a marked decline in the European population in recent times due mainly to habitat changes and use of pesticides.

It is a summer visitor to Europe, the whole population wintering in Africa south of the Sahara, though small numbers may winter in North Africa and parts of the Middle East. It crosses the Mediterranean on a broad front, and is not common at raptor watchpoints. It probably over-flies the Mediterranean and Sahara in a non-stop flight.

Migration: Dispersal from late July with main movements in late August to October, returning in February—April.

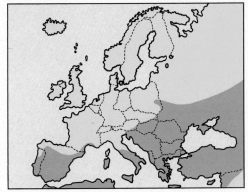

Length:	32 cm
Wing length:	24 cm
Weight:	140 g
Voice:	Hoarse series of calls: 'che-che-che' or 'chit-chit'
Breeding period:	May, 1 brood per year. Replacement clutch possible
Size of clutch:	3–6 (2–8) eggs
Colour of eggs:	Light red-brown with dark brown patches
Size of eggs:	35 × 28 mm
Incubation:	28–29 days, from complete clutch
Fledging period:	Nidicolous; able to fly at 28 days

♀ with prey (agama), Anatolia, 17.6.1977 (Li)

Ad. ♂ carrying prey, Anatolia, 1977 (Li)

Young in eyrie, Anatolia, 17.6.1977 (Li)

) Ad. ♂, Anatolia, Turkey, 1977 (Li)

185

Kestrel (Falco tinnunculus)

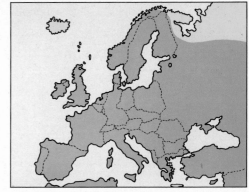

The commonest and most widespread raptor in Europe, found in virtually all types of habitat and altitude.

It feeds mainly on small mammals, though birds, reptiles and insects are also taken. It has a characteristic hunting method of hovering over open ground then dropping on to prey. However, birds are taken in direct flight. It uses a remarkable diversity of nest-sites including holes in trees, cliff-ledges, old buildings, nest-boxes and even on the ground. Old nests of other birds are also used. Little or no nesting material is used in hole- or ledge-nests, but both sexes take part in building tree-nests using twigs, small branches and other vegetation. Incubation is by the ♀ alone. In the early stages the ♂ brings most of the food; later both parents hunt.

The European population has not suffered a major decline, though use of pesticides reduced numbers in the 1960s. Fluctuations in numbers occur due to cyclical abundance of voles and other small mammals.

Northern populations are migratory, wintering from central Europe through Mediterranean countries to tropical Africa. Other populations are only partially migratory or dispersive.

Migration: Mainly late August to November with return in March to early May.

Length:	♂ 32 cm, ♀ 35 cm
Wing length:	♂ 25 cm, ♀ 26 cm
Weight:	♂ 220 g, ♀ 230 g
Voice:	Loud-yelling 'kee-kee-kee', 'kick, kick'
Breeding period:	Beginning of April to June, 1 brood per year. Replacement clutch possible
Size of clutch:	3–6 (1–9) eggs
Colour of eggs:	Yellowish white, with thick reddish markings
Size of eggs:	42 × 35 mm
Incubation:	27–29 days
Fledging period:	Nidicolous; able to fly at 27–32 days. ♂♂ developing more quickly than ♀♀

eyrie in a building, La Crau, France, 1967 (Li)

Imm., Greece, 18.8.1977 (Pf)

Bavaria, 15.5.1975 (Pf)

) ♂ brings prey to nest, Bavaria, West Germany, 1975 (Li)

Willow Grouse (Lagopus lagopus)

The Willow Grouse is the Continental form of the species which has a white winter plumage. The British and Irish race is known as Red Grouse (*Lagopus lagopus scoticus*) and keeps its red-brown plumage through the year.

It is a bird of open moorland, tundra, heath and bogs, feeding entirely on vegetation such as heather shoots, catkins, buds and other low plants depending on range.

It nests in thick vegetation, often lining the scrape with scraps of vegetation or peat. Incubation is entirely by the ♀, while the ♂ stands guard nearby. Often remains in family groups after breeding season, but will form flocks in winter.

Populations fluctuate cyclicly, and in some areas there has been a decline in population. It has been introduced successfully in some places, including south-west England.

It is a resident species, British birds rarely moving more than 10 km from nesting areas, though the most northerly European population may move further south in extreme winters.

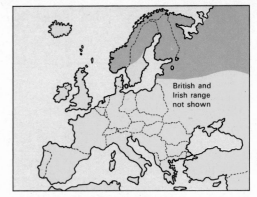

British and Irish range not shown

Length:	♂ 40 cm, ♀ 38 cm
Wing length:	♂ 20 cm, ♀ 19 cm
Weight:	♂ 680 g, ♀ 580 g
Voice:	Hoarse, far-carrying calls: 'goh wa', 'kok-kok-kok-krrr'
Breeding period:	Beginning of May to July, 1 brood per year. Replacement clutch possible
Size of clutch:	6–10 (2–17) eggs
Colour of eggs:	Yellow-brown, with plentiful black patches
Size of eggs:	46 × 32 mm
Incubation:	19–25 days, beg. when clutch complete
Fledging period:	Nidifugous; able to fly at 12–13 days

nsitional plumage, mid-Norway, 3.6.1965 (Sy)

r) Brooding ♀, central Norway, 24.6.1968 (Sy)

Chicks, Finnish Lapland (Pl)

Willow Grouse's eggs, laid in captivity (Pf)

189

Ptarmigan (Lagopus mutus)

The Ptarmigan inhabits high mountainous regions, above the treeline, also frequenting tundra to sea level in the north of its range. It is normally found at higher altitudes than the Red Grouse. It feeds entirely on plant matter, heather, bilberry, dwarf willows and other low plants. The nest is on the ground, a shallow scrape sometimes lined with a little grass or other vegetation. It is often sited near a large stone or low scrub, though sometimes completely in the open. Incubation is by the ♀ alone, with the ♂ standing guard. After hatching the ♂♂ usually desert leaving the ♀♀ to rear the young, the ♀♀ and young remaining in a family group sometimes joined by other ♀♀ and young to form a crèche.

The species is basically resident, though it often descends to lower altitude in winter. Birds in the extreme north of the range disperse more widely in winter.

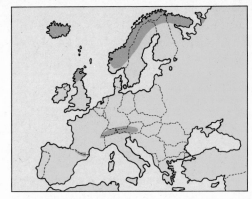

Length:	35 cm
Wing length:	♂ 20 cm, ♀ 19 cm
Weight:	450 g
Voice:	Courtship call: hoarse, wooden scraping 'arrrrrh'. In flight: 'arr-a-ka-ka'
Breeding period:	Mid-May, beginning of August, 1 brood per year. Replacement clutch probable
Size of clutch:	5–8 (3–12) eggs
Colour of eggs:	Cream to reddish brown, with large and small patches
Size of eggs:	43 × 30 mm
Incubation:	21–23 days, beginning from last egg
Fledging period:	Nidifugous; able to fly at *ca* 10 days. Independent at about 3 months

...nigan ♂, Finnish Lapland (Pl)

Ptarmigan in winter plumage, ♂ left, ♀ right (Li)

Young, being reared in captivity (Pf)

Ptarmigan clutch, laid in captivity (Pf).

191

Black Grouse (Tetrao tetrix)

The Black Grouse frequents areas where forest or woodland meet heath-land, bog or open country. It feeds on shoots, catkins, berries and some insects, the diet depending on main plant species in breeding area. In the early spring groups of ♂♂ collect at lekking grounds to display. These leks are usually traditional and are often sited in peat bogs. Several ♂♂ will perform a complex display often involving fighting. Dominant ♂♂ will mate with onlooking ♀♀. There is no pair-bond and a ♂ may mate with several ♀♀. The nest is on the ground in the shelter of vegetation. The ♀ incubates and rears the young alone.

Outside the breeding season the ♀♀ and young may flock, the ♂♂ flocking throughout much of the year.

The species has decreased in numbers and range throughout most of Europe except for the northern part of the range. This decrease is probably due mainly to habitat changes.

It is largely resident, though the ♀♀ and young ♂♂ may wander short distances in winter. In the northern part of the range longer movements are known up to 1000 km.

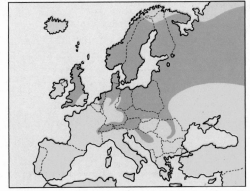

Length:	♂ 55 cm, ♀ 40 cm
Wing length:	♂ 26 cm, ♀ 23 cm
Weight:	♂ ca 1200 g, ♀ ca 900 g
Voice:	♂ at lek 'roo-oo-roo', 'to-wha', 'whushee'. Hen: 'chuck-chuck'
Breeding period:	May–June, 1 brood per year. Replacement clutch possible
Size of clutch:	7–10 (3–16) eggs
Colour of eggs:	Ochre, with red-brown patches
Size of eggs:	50 × 36 mm
Incubation:	26–27 days, beginning from last egg
Fledging period:	Nidifugous; capable of flight from ca 12 days, independent at about 3 months

♀, Bavaria, 1975 (Li)

) Displaying ♂, Bavarian Alps, West Germany, 25.5.1975 (Li)

8-day-old birds, Bavarian forest, 20.5.1975 (Pf)

Bavarian forest, 12.5.1973 (Pf)

193

Capercaillie (Tetrao urogallus)

The Capercaillie is the largest and most arboreal of the grouse. It is found in forested areas, both lowland and montane, preferring ancient woodland with areas of bilberry. In winter it feeds mainly on pine-needles and shoots, in summer it takes leaves, stem and berries of bilberry and other plants. Insect food is also taken and is an important part of the diet for chicks.

The ♂♂ have an impressive display and are very aggressive, some even towards human intruders in the territory. Dominant ♂♂ will mate with many ♀♀ who incubate and rear the young alone. The nest is on the ground in dense cover, typically at the base of a tree. Rarely, the nest of another species may be used up to 5 m from the ground.

There has been a marked decline in the European population mainly due to felling of forests, shooting and climatic changes. The species became extinct in Scotland in the late 1700s and was reintroduced in the mid-1800s onwards.

The species is largely resident throughout the European range.

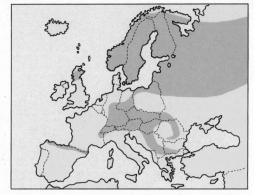

Length:	♂ 85 cm, ♀ 62 cm
Wing length:	♂ 39 cm, ♀ 30 cm
Weight:	♂ 4000 g, ♀ 1800 g
Voice:	♂ song: 'Telip, telip, telip, tip-tip-tip-t-t-khop'. Hen: 'kock-kock'
Breeding period:	Mid-April to mid-June, 1 brood per year. Replacement clutch possible
Size of clutch:	6–10 (4–16) eggs
Colour of eggs:	Yellowish rusty brown, with fine dark red patches and spots
Size of eggs:	57 × 41 mm
Incubation:	24–26 days, from complete clutch
Fledging period:	Nidifugous; able to fly at 2 weeks, remaining with the ♀ until autumn

♀, Austria, 1975 (Li)

3-day-old chick, 29.5.1975 (Pf)

Bavarian forest, 20.5.1975 (Pf)

) Adult ♂ displaying, Bavaria, West Germany, 1960 (Li)

Hazel Grouse (Bonasa bonasia)

The Hazel Grouse inhabits mixed forest with conifers, deciduous trees and a good understory. It is mainly vegetarian, taking a variety of leaves, shoots, berries and seeds. It also takes insects, which are the main food of the chicks. In winter it is mainly an arboreal feeder, becoming terrestrial in summer. The nest is a shallow scrape, usually well concealed by vegetation and often under a low bush or tree. Incubation is by the ♀ alone, the ♂ standing guard nearby. ♂♂ may also join the ♀ and brood after hatching.

The species has decreased greatly in most of west and central Europe, probably as a result of hunting and habitat changes. In the north of its range the population is more stable.

Hazel Grouse are the most sedentary of the European grouse: some ♀♀ may move locally in autumn but ♂♂ set up territory in autumn, so movements are rare.

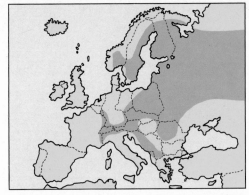

Length:	35–36 cm
Wing length:	17 cm
Weight:	400 g
Voice:	Courting: ♂ a thin, high whistle: 'tsee-tsee, tsitseritsi, tswitsi'. ♀ 'plit-plit'
Breeding period:	End of April, May, 1 brood per year. Replacement clutch possible
Size of clutch:	7–11 eggs
Colour of eggs:	Cream with small brown spots
Size of eggs:	41 × 29 mm
Incubation:	22–27 days, from complete clutch
Fledging period:	Nidifugous; independent at ca 3 months

ubating ♀ (Sa)

°) Ad. ♂, Bavarian forest, West Germany (St)

Hazel Grouse chick, 9 days old, Bavarian forest (Dr A)

Bavarian forest, 29.5.1971 (Pf)

Rock Partridge (Alectoris graeca)

The Rock Partridge inhabits dry mountainous areas in south-east Europe. It is found in open woodland, though it prefers low scrub, heathland and meadows as well as rocky ground. The nest is on the ground often in the shelter of a rock or in vegetation. Incubation is by the ♀ alone but the ♂ broods a second clutch. The pair-bond is strong and often long-lasting. Outside the breeding season the species forms coveys or quite large flocks, with up to a hundred individuals recorded. Unpaired ♂♂ flock together in summer.

The diet is mainly leaves, buds, seeds and shoots of low plants, though insects are also taken and form the main diet of chicks.

The Rock Partridge is replaced by the Red-legged Partridge (*Alectoris rufa*) in western Europe, though this species prefers lowland habitats.

Both species are hunted and stock is introduced into many areas for hunting purposes. Both species are sedentary.

Length:	33–35 cm
Wing length:	16–17 cm
Weight:	500–650 g
Voice:	Courting: 'tit-tit-chik', or Nuthatch-like 'vit-vit'. At take-off, a whistling 'pee-yoo'
Breeding period:	Beginning of May, June, one or two broods. Replacement clutch possible
Size of clutch:	9–14 (6–18) eggs
Colour of eggs:	Light mud colour with small red-brown spots and larger patches
Size of eggs:	41 × 30 mm
Incubation:	24–26 days, beginning from last egg
Fledging period:	Nidifugous; able to fly at *ca* 7–10 days

ith chicks (Li)

) Ad. ♂ (Li)

Rock Partridge chicks, 1 day old (Pf)

Rock Partridge nest and eggs (Li)

Partridge (Perdix perdix)

The Partridge is found mainly in agricultural habitats especially where cover in the form of woodland, hedges or rough vegetation provide suitable nesting sites. The nest is on the ground in dense vegetation and is a hollow lined with grass and a few feathers built by the ♀. The ♀ broods alone, though the ♂ may stand guard and help to rear the young, even brooding the first hatched chicks while the ♀ sits on the remaining eggs.

The diet is chiefly plant matter including shoots, grass, seeds and grain. Insects are also taken and are the main diet of young chicks.

After the breeding season parents and young form coveys and may remain in family groups till spring.

Modern agricultural methods involving clearing hedges and other cover has led to a decrease in population in parts of the range. The species is hunted extensively and some protection is afforded by game management. Partridges are mainly resident, though eastern European birds are partially migratory.

Length:	30 cm
Wing length:	15 cm
Weight:	300–400 g
Voice:	'Girr-reck', on take-off 'reck-reck-reck'
Breeding period:	April–June, 1 brood per year. Replacement clutch possible
Size of clutch:	10–12 (8–24) eggs
Colour of eggs:	Olive or mud-colour
Size of eggs:	35 × 27 mm
Incubation:	24–26 days, beginning from last egg
Fledging period:	Nidifugous; able to fly at 2 weeks

♀, Odenwald, Hessen, West Germany, 4.2.1964 (Pf)

11-day-old chicks, Bavaria, 12.5.1977 (Pf)

Seewinkel, Austria, 1963 (Li)

*) ♂ leading young, Bavaria, West Germany (Li)

Quail (Coturnix coturnix)

The Quail is found in open areas, particularly agricultural land with growing crops; it avoids woodlands or unvegetated ground. It breeds over a wide area in Europe but is subject to fluctuations in both range and numbers. It appears to have decreased severely in some parts of its range, perhaps due to the very large numbers that are taken by hunters along the Mediterranean coasts when it is on migration.

It feeds on seeds of a variety of plants and also on insects, particularly ants, beetles and bugs.

The nest is on the ground, usually in dense cover, and is a scrape made by the ♀ and lined with grass or other plant materials. The ♀ incubates alone and rears the young. ♂♂ may be monogamous, polygamous or promiscuous depending on the sex ratio in the area.

Quail are mainly migratory: some winter in Iberia and North Africa but most migrate to spend the winter in tropical Africa, crossing the Sahara in one flight. When returning to Europe in spring the species is prone to overshooting its normal range during warm weather. This often results in calling birds and nesting outside the normal range.

Migration: Mainly September to early November, returning in April to May. Also into June in north of range.

Length:	17–18 cm
Wing length:	11 cm
Weight:	90 g
Voice:	'Pick-perwick', also a ventriloquist-like 'veveck veveck'
Breeding period:	April–June, 1 brood. Replacements frequent
Size of clutch:	7–12 (6–18) eggs
Colour of eggs:	Sandy, with dark patches
Size of eggs:	30 × 23 mm
Incubation:	18–21 days, beginning from last egg
Fledging period:	Nidifugous; able to fly at 19 days. Independent at 4–7 weeks

1-day-old chick (Pf)

Bavaria, West Germany, 16.6.1975 (Pf)

nest (Pf)

) Ad. ♂ (Pf)

Pheasant (Phasianus colchicus)

The Pheasant is a native of Asia, introduced into Europe from Roman times and the Middle Ages. Frequent reintroductions and game management have resulted in it being a common bird in farmland and low-lying woodland throughout much of Europe. It feeds on a variety of plant matter including grain, seeds, fruits and nuts, as well as insects and occasionally small vertebrates.

The nest is on the ground, usually in thick vegetation, and is a scrape lined with grass by the ♀. It is the ♀ that incubates and rears the young. Though some ♂♂ are monogamous, many have a harem of several ♀♀. Outside the breeding season the species will form flocks, which may be of both or separate sexes.

It is essentially resident, though slight local movement occurs to exploit the best feeding areas.

It is an important gamebird throughout Europe. Interbreeding with Green Pheasant *P. versicolor* and mixing of various races has resulted in a number of variant plumages.

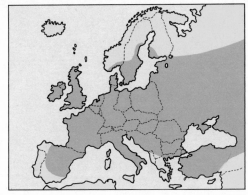

Length:	♂ 80 cm, ♀ 60 cm
Wing length:	♂ 25 cm, ♀ 22 cm
Weight:	♂ 1400 g, ♀ 1200 g
Voice:	Double call, 'cuccuck'. Hen: a light whistle
Breeding period:	March–June, 1 brood per year. Replacement clutches frequent
Size of clutch:	8–12 (6–16) eggs
Colour of eggs:	Olive-brown to blue-grey
Size of eggs:	46 × 36 mm
Incubation:	23–28 days, beginning from last egg
Fledging period:	Nidifugous; able to fly at 2 weeks, independent at 11 weeks

id ♂, Bavaria, 1.6.1962 (Pf)

Juv., Bavaria, 1976 (Li)

Chicks hatching, Bavaria, 18.5.1977 (Pf)

Displaying ♂ with ♀, Bavaria, West Germany, end of April 1974 (Mo)

205

Crane (Grus grus)

Cranes inhabit wetlands, marshes, swampy woodlands and the margins of reedy lakes. They take a wide variety of food, mainly plant material including roots, seeds, leaves and fruits; animal prey includes insects, snails, small mammals, amphibians and reptiles.

Cranes are monogamous and pair for life. They have a spectacular dancing display which may involve lone birds or flocks.

The nest is a large pile of vegetation sited in an inaccessible spot, often on a mound or hummock surrounded by bog. Both sexes share in nest-building, incubation (though the ♀ takes the larger part) and rearing of young. The parents and young remain together as a family group through the winter.

Cranes are migratory, wintering in Iberia, North Africa, Turkey and the Middle East, some moving as far as Sudan and Ethiopia. They migrate in flocks along a narrow front with traditional stopping-off points *en route*.

Migration: Autumn movements in September–November, return passage in March and April.

Length:	♂:120 cm, ♀ 110 cm
Wing length:	♂ 59 cm, ♀ 56 cm
Weight:	♂ 5500 g, ♀ 4850 g
Voice:	Far-carrying trumpeting, 'krooh krooh'
Breeding period:	May–June, 1 brood per year. Replacement clutch possible
Size of clutch:	2 (1–3) eggs
Colour of eggs:	Grey-green to reddish brown, brown spots
Size of eggs:	97 × 62 mm
Incubation:	28–30 days, beginning from last egg
Fledging period:	Nidifugous; able to fly at 65–70 days

ne, landing (*G. g. lilfordi*), Anatolia, 28.5.1975 (Li)

Chick, central Sweden, 16.6.1968 (Sy)

Anatolia, 14.6.1973 (Li)

) (*Grus grus lilfordi*), Anatolia, Turkey, 28.5.1975 (Li)

Water Rail (Rallus aquaticus)

Water Rails are secretive birds living in marshes, swamps, margins of rivers and lakes and other wetland with dense vegetation. They are omnivorous, taking all manner of insects, invertebrates, small fish and amphibians. Plant matter, carrion and small birds are also taken.

The nest is usually sited in dense cover, often in reeds, and is a sturdy cup of reeds and leaves built by both sexes. The ♀ does most of the incubation and both parents share in rearing the young.

Though resident over much of its range including Iceland, birds from parts of Scandinavia and eastern Europe migrate to Britain, France and parts of western Europe. Some birds move as far as North Africa and the species also winters in the Middle East. In winter it may be found in more open habitats, and is not shy of man. It will feed in similar situations to the Moorhen, particularly in hard weather.

Migration: Dispersal from July, with main movements in September–November. Return passage in March and April.

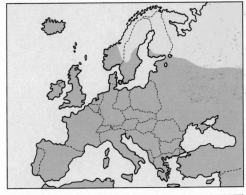

Length:	28 cm
Wing length:	♂ 12 cm, ♀ 11 cm
Weight:	*ca* 115 g
Voice:	'Crueeh-crueeh-crueeh', reminiscent of a squeaking piglet
Breeding period:	April–July, 2 broods per year
Size of clutch:	6–10 (5–12) eggs
Colour of eggs:	Cream with dark spots
Size of eggs:	36 × 26 mm
Incubation:	19–20 days, beg. when clutch complete
Fledging period:	Nidifugous, but attended in the nest for a few days. Able to fly at *ca* 25 days. Independent at 7 weeks

m., Bavaria, West Germany, September 1976 (Zei)

ft) Seewinkel, Austria, 1970 (Li)

Chick, 10 days old, Bavaria, 13.5.1974 (Pf)

Clutch in which a Pheasant has 'dumped' two eggs, Bavaria, 9.5.1975 (Pf)

Spotted Crake (Porzana porzana)

The Spotted Crake is a shy, secretive inhabitant of fens, marshes and similar wetlands: It is difficult to observe, and often the only clue to its presence is the distinctive call. It feeds on small aquatic creatures including molluscs, insects and larvae. It also takes a variety of plant matter, particularly seeds.

The nest is usually close to the water in dense cover, and it is a substantial cup of dead leaves and other vegetation built by both sexes. Incubation is shared by both parents as is the care of the young.

Though a few birds overwinter in Europe, the species is mainly migratory, wintering in eastern Africa south of the Sahara. Juvenile birds will remain off-passage at certain sites in August whilst they moult.

Migration: Dispersal from July, main passage late August to November, returning in March and April.

The breeding distribution in Europe is not well known due to the difficulty of proving breeding and to birds calling while still on passage. The area shown on the map is a rough guide.

Length:	23 cm
Wing length:	12 cm
Weight:	80 g
Voice:	Courting call of ♂ a high, sharp, 'hwit, hwit' (reminiscent of a whip-lash)
Breeding period:	Mid-April, beginning of June, usually 2 broods. Replacement clutch possible
Size of clutch:	8–12 (6–14) eggs
Colour of eggs:	Cream with reddish brown patches
Size of eggs:	33 × 24 mm
Incubation:	18–21 days, from second or third egg
Fledging period:	Nidifugous; able to fly at 25–30 days

Incomplete clutch, Lower Saxony, June 1968 (Di)

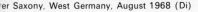

er Saxony, West Germany, August 1968 (Di)

Bavaria, West Germany, August 1975 (Zei)

211

Moorhen (Gallinula chloropus)

The Moorhen is a common inhabitant of inland waters and wetland of most types. It requires less vegetation than the smaller crakes and rails. It is quite arboreal and will nest in waterside trees. It swims freely and obtains much of its food while swimming. It eats a variety of plant matter including pondweeds, seeds and leaves. Animal matter is also taken (insects, aquatic invertebrates, small fish and amphibians).

Nest-sites are varied, ranging from reedbeds and similar emergent vegetation to floating nests, nests in trees and low bushes or on branches in the water. The nest is built by both sexes and is a cup of leaves, stems, twigs and reeds. Incubation and care of the young is also done by both sexes and the young of the first brood may help to feed those of the second. Birds from the western and southern parts of Europe are largely resident, but birds from the north and east of the range migrate. They winter in western Europe, North Africa and the Middle East, though some reach tropical Africa.

Migration: Dispersal from July with main movements in September—November. Spring passage in March and April.

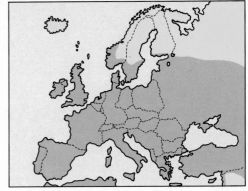

Length:	33 cm
Wing length:	18 cm
Weight:	300 g
Voice:	Scraping 'crerk' or 'curruk', 'kitick', etc.
Breeding period:	April—July, 2–3 broods per year
Size of clutch:	5–10 (2–20) eggs
Colour of eggs:	Buff with dark spots
Size of eggs:	43 × 31 mm
Incubation:	19–22 days
Fledging period:	Nidifugous; but attended for a few days in the nest. Independent at 5 weeks

1-day-old chick, Bavaria, 24.5.1977 (Pf)

Bavaria, end of April 1977 (Pf)

...varia, July 1965 (Li)

...) Ad. with chicks, Bavaria, West Germany, July 1965 (Li)

213

Coot (Fulica atra)

Coot are widespread on lakes, slow rivers, reservoirs, lagoons and even ornamental waters in urban situations. They are omnivorous, taking mainly plant material, including terrestrial plants, insects, aquatic invertebrates and, to a lesser extent, small fish, mammals and amphibians.

The nest-site is usually in shallow water, often concealed by reeds or other vegetation. The nest is a bulky cup of reedstems and other plant material, built by both sexes, though the ♂ brings most material for the ♀ to add to structure. Both sexes share incubation and care of the young. Outside the breeding season the species is gregarious and large numbers concentrate on suitable waters which may include brackish or even sheltered marine waters.

The northern and eastern populations are migratory, wintering in western Europe, North Africa and the Middle East.

Migration: Mainly September–November, returning in March and April.

The Crested Coot (*Fulica cristata*) is a rare resident in south-west Spain. It inhabits similar waters to the Coot but has decreased so much in recent years that it faces extinction in Europe.

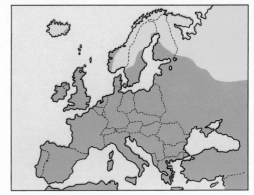

Length:	38 cm
Wing length:	20 cm
Weight:	800 g
Voice:	Barking 'kowk, kewk', or a sharp 'pix'
Breeding period:	March–July, 1–2 broods per year. Replacements possible
Size of clutch:	7–9 (5–15) eggs, over 14 result from 2 ♀♀
Colour of eggs:	Yellowish brown, with black spots
Size of eggs:	52 × 36 mm
Incubation:	21–24 days, beginning from second egg
Fledging period:	Nidifugous; but brooded in the nest for 3–4 days. Independent at 8 weeks

1-day-old chick, Bavaria, July 1977 (Pf)

Bavaria, 1970 (Li)

aria, May 1958 (Pf)

♀) Bavaria, West Germany, March 1974 (Li)

Great Bustard (Otis tarda)

Once widespread over much of Europe the species is now found only in south-west and eastern Europe, where it is endangered. The decrease in population is due mainly to changes in habitat as a result of agricultural pressures, hunting and use of pesticides.

Great Bustards like open, undulating country and require an unobscured view of at least 1 km from the nest-site.

Incubation is by the ♀ alone; ♂♂ may be polygamous or promiscuous. The ♂♂ have elaborate display and form leks on traditional displaying grounds. After mating they remain in flocks, there being no pair-bond. Outside the breeding season the species is gregarious, flocks occurring wherever there are suitable feeding areas.

The diet consists of a variety of plant matter including shoots, leaves and flowers, with an increasing tendency to feed on crops such as Brassica, especially in hard winters. Animal materials taken mainly in summer, include large insects, small mammals, amphibians and reptiles.

The species is not truly migratory except for easternmost populations but is subject to hard-weather movements which may take the form of an 'invasion' to west European countries including Britain.

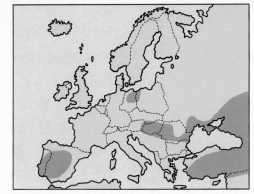

Length:	♂ 102 cm, ♀ 76 cm
Wing length:	♂ 63 cm, ♀ 49 cm
Weight:	♂ 11,500 g, ♀ 4500 g
Voice:	Displaying ♂ produces 'ump-ump' sound from inflated gular sac, also 'uck' and other short calls. Silent outside breeding season
Breeding period:	End of April to July, 1 brood per year. Replacement clutch possible
Size of clutch:	2–3 (1) eggs
Colour of eggs:	Grey-green to olive brown, with smeary brown patches
Size of eggs:	80 × 57 mm
Incubation:	21–28 days, from first or second egg
Fledging period:	Nidifugous; able to fly at ca 5 weeks

♀, Institute for Comparative Ethology, Vienna (Li)

Displaying ♂, Institute for Comparative Ethology, Vienna (Li)

Feeding on cabbages, winter 1963. Marchfield, Austria (Fe)

Seewinkel, Austria, 1968 (Li)

Little Bustard (Tetrax tetrax)

The Little Bustard frequents open or undulating country with low, scrubby vegetation. It is also found to some extent in western Europe in agricultural land with crops such as clover or lucerne.

It feeds mainly on plant matter such as shoots, leaves, grain and flowers, and also takes a variety of invertebrates, particularly grasshoppers and beetles.

The nest is a scrape, often in low vegetation, and the ♀ may partly cover herself with scraps of plant matter for further camouflage during incubation. The ♀ incubates and rears the young alone. The ♂♂ lek and have an elaborate display. Outside the breeding season the species is gregarious, often occurring in large flocks, with up to 1000 recorded.

It is migratory over much of the range and a partial migrant in the more southern areas. Large numbers are found in La Crau in Southern France and also in south-west Spain.

The species suffered a decline in parts of its range but the western European population seems to be fairly stable, even increasing in some areas.

Migration: Dispersal in autumn from August continuing to December, spring movements in March and April.

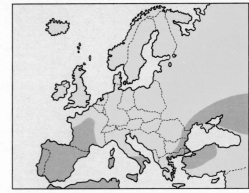

Length:	40–45 cm
Wing length:	♂ 25 cm, ♀ 24.5 cm
Weight:	About 900 g
Voice:	♂ courting calls, grating 'prrit' and 'ogh'. ♀ mostly mute, but when disturbed a trilling 'Tr-rr'
Breeding period:	End of April, May, June, 1 brood per year. Replacement clutch even in July
Size of clutch:	3–4 (2–5) eggs
Colour of eggs:	Olive-green to olive-brown, with brown streaks and blotches
Size of eggs:	52 × 38 mm
Incubation:	20–21 days
Fledging period:	Nidifugous; able to fly at 3–4 weeks

♂ in breeding plumage (O.v.F.)

6-day-old chick, La Crau, South of France (O.v.F.)

4-week-old chick, photographed in reservation (O.v.F.)

La Crau, 19.6.1978 (O.v.F.)

Oystercatcher (Haematopus ostralegus)

The Oystercatcher is found on shingle and sandy beaches along coasts and rivers. It is also found inland in some areas of grassland, agricultural land and moor or heathlands. The nest is a scrape sometimes lined with pieces of vegetation, small stones or other debris. Incubation is by both sexes, as is care of the young. The young remain near the nest at first and are fed by the parents.

The food is mainly molluscs, crustaceans, worms and insects. Food is often obtained on the shore but it will feed inland on soft ground, ploughed fields and the like. Contrary to its name, the species does not take oysters, though it skilfully opens other bivalves with its strong bill. In the north of its range the species is migratory, wintering in western Europe, the Mediterranean region and the African coast.

Migration: July—November in autumn, returning in March—April.

Length:	43 cm
Wing length:	25 cm
Weight:	500 g
Voice:	Call 'pik-pik' or 'kleep kleep'; in a trilling series at courtship
Breeding period:	Mid-April, June, 1 brood per year. Replacement clutch possible
Size of clutch:	3 (2–4) eggs
Colour of eggs:	Buffish-yellow with dark spots or irregular blotches
Size of eggs:	56 × 40 mm
Incubation:	24–27 days, beg. from complete clutch
Fledging period:	Nidifugous; but remaining 1–2 days in the nest. Independent at 6 weeks

way, June 1974 (Mo)

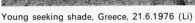

) Changing places on the nest, Greece, 40.5.1972 (Li)

Young seeking shade, Greece, 21.6.1976 (Li)

Greece, 30.5.1972 (Li)

221

Spur-winged Plover

(Hoplopterus spinosus)

The Spur-winged Plover is a very scarce breeding bird in the south-east of the region. It is found in open areas with sparse vegetation, particularly mud or sandbanks on large rivers and lakes, estuaries and river deltas and in growing crops.

The nest is a scrape in open ground decorated with scraps of plant material. Both sexes incubate and help to rear the young. The diet includes worms, molluscs and insects though it has not been well studied in Europe.

The species is migratory, wintering in Africa and parts of the Middle East. The Spur-winged Plover was only recently added to the list of European breeding birds when it was found nesting in north-east Greece. It is mainly found in Ethiopian Africa and the Middle East.

Migration: Autumn passage mostly September—October, returning in March and April.

Length:	28 cm
Wing length:	20 cm
Weight:	170 g
Voice:	Metallic 'pit-pit', scratching 'zeet-zeet-zeet' and noisy 'zikzak zikzak'
Breeding period:	End of April, May, 1 brood per year. Replacement clutch and second brood possible
Size of clutch:	4 (2–5) eggs
Colour of eggs:	Olive-green with dark patches and spots
Size of eggs:	41 × 28 mm
Incubation:	21–25 days, beg. from complete clutch
Fledging period:	Nidifugous; other information lacking

. crouching, northern Greece, 16.6.1976 (Li)

) Changing places on the nest, northern Greece, 30.5.1972 (Li)

1-day-old chick, Cilicia, Turkey, 16.5.1975 (Li)

Northern Greece, 30.5.1972 (Li)

Lapwing (Vanellus vanellus)

One of the commonest waders of Europe, the Lapwing breeds in a variety of habitats including agricultural land, damp meadows and marshland. It is a conspicuous bird with a noisy acrobatic display flight. The nest is a scrape usually lined with grass or other plant matter, sometimes built up to form a substantial cup. Incubation is by both sexes but the ♀ takes the larger share. The young are tended by both parents though the ♂ tends to guard while the ♀ feeds the young.

The diet is chiefly insects, worms, some molluscs and plant matter, mostly seeds.

Birds from the northern part of the range are migratory, moving to western Europe, North Africa and parts of the Middle East in winter. Outside the breeding season it is markedly gregarious and large flocks occur on suitable habitat. Hard weather often results in large-scale movements throughout the winter.

Migration: Dispersal in autumn from July onwards, mainly August—November, returning in late February to April.

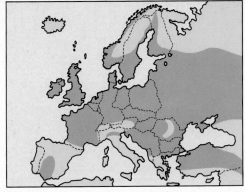

Length:	30 cm
Wing length:	21 cm
Weight:	200 g
Voice:	'Pee-wit, pee-wit', throbbing wing noise at courtship
Breeding period:	End of March, May, 1 brood per year. Replacement clutch possible
Size of clutch:	4 (2–5) eggs
Colour of eggs:	Variable olive-green to greyish yellow, with dark flecks
Size of eggs:	47 × 34 mm
Incubation:	25–30 days, beg. from complete clutch
Fledging period:	Nidifugous; independent at ca 4 weeks

Young crouching, Bavaria, 1973 (Li)

Bavaria, beginning of April 1975 (Pf)

...varia, May 1975 (Pf)

...ft) Seewinkel, Austria, 1962 (Li)

225

Ringed Plover (Charadrius hiaticula)

The Ringed Plover is found mainly on shingle or sandy shores. It also occurs on lake and river-banks and in the north of its range will be found far inland breeding on heath or moorland. The nest is a scrape in open ground, sometimes in the shelter of a low plant or rocks. It is lined with small stones or plant materials. Incubation is by both sexes, the young are able to feed themselves soon after leaving the nest.

'Injury-feigning' or the 'broken-wing trick' is of common occurrence during the breeding season to decoy predators or intruders away from the nest.

The food consists of small molluscs, insects, invertebrates and some plant material.

Northern populations are migratory, moving to the coasts of western Europe, the Middle East and as far as South Africa. The species is almost entirely coastal in winter, favouring muddy shores where molluscs and marine invertebrates abound.

Migration: Autumn passage from July to October, returning in February—April.

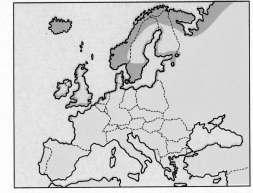

Length:	19 cm
Wing length:	13 cm
Weight:	60 g
Voice:	A melodious 'too-i' or in series 'tooloolooloo'
Breeding period:	May, July, 1–2 broods per year, sometimes 3
Size of clutch:	4 (3–5) eggs
Colour of eggs:	Very variable, sandy to blue-grey with dark spots
Size of eggs:	36 × 26 mm
Incubation:	23–27 days
Fledging period:	Nidifugous; independent at 3 weeks

't bird decoying, Amrum, North Sea, May 1966 (Qu)
Öland, Sweden, 1973 (Mo)

Migrant, Bavaria, West Germany, September 1975 (Pf)

Chicks and eggs, Öland, Sweden, May 1973 (Par)

Little Ringed Plover

(Charadrius dubius)

The Little Ringed Plover frequents inland areas such as river banks, lakes and gravel-pits wherever large areas of shingle or gravel occur. The nest is a scrape usually in gravel or sand but sometimes on dry mud or amongst low vegetation. The scrape is sometimes lined with small stones or scraps of plant material. Incubation is by both sexes who also share in the care of the young. Food is mainly insects, invertebrates, molluscs and sometimes worms.

The species has colonised Britain from the 1940s and has bred as far north as Scotland. It generally prefers a warmer climate to the Ringed Plover and is not found in the far north. The spread of the species in the northern parts of its range is closely linked with sand or gravel extraction, providing a habitat that was previously lacking.

Little Ringed Plovers are almost entirely migratory: a few winter in Mediterranean countries but most move to Africa from Morocco south to the Equator.

Migration: Autumn movement from July to October, spring passage in March—May.

Length:	15 cm
Wing length:	11 cm
Weight:	40—45 g
Voice:	'Pee-oo'. Courtship: 'gee-a, gee-a'
Breeding period:	April, June, 2 broods per year in south
Size of clutch:	4 (3—5) eggs
Colour of eggs:	Whitish grey or sandy, with dark spots or patches
Size of eggs:	30 × 22 mm
Incubation:	24—26 days, beg. from complete clutch
Fledging period:	Nidifugous; independent at 3 weeks

Seewinkel, Austria, 1961 (Li)

♂) Ad. ♂, Bavaria, West Germany, 6.5.1974 (Pf)

Chicks, Bavaria, 20.5.1970 (Pf)

Bavaria, 6.4.1971 (Pf)

Kentish Plover (Charadrius alexandrinus)

The Kentish Plover prefers warmer, dryer areas than the Ringed Plover. It is found chiefly on coastal areas with mud, shingle or sand, but will also frequent inland seas and lagoons and areas of dry mud with sparse vegetation near water. The nest is sited in the open and is a scrape, sometimes lined with scraps of plant matter; the eggs are often half-buried in sand.

The food is similar to that of the Ringed Plover, with insects predominating.

The European population is partially migratory; birds from the north of the range winter from the Mediterranean to South Africa. The more southerly breeding birds are probably resident. It is mainly coastal in winter and is rarely seen inland even on passage.

Migration: Autumn movements from late July to October with return in March—May.

The species has always been a scarce breeding bird in Britain, and no nests were known from the late 1950s till quite recently.

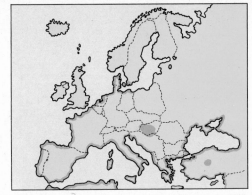

Length:	16 cm
Wing length:	11 cm
Weight:	40 g
Voice:	Gentle 'pwit-pwit', 'trrr' or 'gi-lick'
Breeding period:	April–July, usually 2 broods per year
Size of clutch:	3 (2–4) eggs
Colour of eggs:	Sandy to olive-brown, with fine dark spots and lines
Size of eggs:	33 × 23 mm
Incubation:	23–27 days, beg. from complete clutch
Fledging period:	Nidifugous; independent at 3 weeks

...oding ♀, Central Anatolia, Turkey, 24.5.1974 (Pf)

...) ♂ on nest, Neusiedler See, Austria, 1972 (Mo)

Chicks crouching, Anatolia, 8.5.1974 (Li)

Anatolia, 23.5.1974 (Li)

Golden Plover (Pluvialis apricaria)

The Golden Plover is a bird of the northern heaths and moorlands, often in upland areas. The nest is a shallow scrape usually lined with moss, lichen or other plant material, usually in the open among short vegetation. Both sexes incubate but mainly the ♀. The diet is very similar to that of the Lapwing, especially in winter when the two species often associate. In summer a variety of insects, invertebrates, worms, seeds and berries are taken.

Outside Britain the species is entirely migratory, and birds from parts of Britain move out in winter. The main wintering areas are in western Europe and North Africa. It is particularly fond of short grasslands especially near the coast or by large rivers. It will also resort to coastal mudflats. It is highly gregarious outside the breeding season and large flocks are seen on passage and in the wintering area.

Migration: Autumn dispersal from July, often halting to moult, continuing to November. Return passage in March–May.

Length:	28 cm
Wing length:	18 cm
Weight:	200 g
Voice:	Call a fluting 'tlu-tee'. Display: 'too-roo too-roo', gently trilling
Breeding period:	End of April, June, 1 brood per year. Replacement clutch possible
Size of clutch:	4 (3) eggs
Colour of eggs:	Sandy to red-brown, heavily blotched mostly at larger end
Size of eggs:	52 × 35 mm
Incubation:	27–28 days, beginning from third egg
Fledging period:	Nidifugous; independent at 4 weeks

n., Amrum, North Sea, September 1973 (Qu)

Chick, Öland, Sweden (Pl)

North Jutland, Denmark, June 1965 (Qu)

t) Ad. in breeding plumage, Öland, Sweden, 1973 (Mo)

233

Dotterel (Eudromias morinellus)

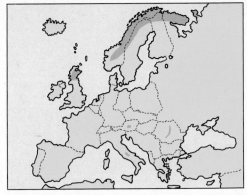

The Dotterel is a bird of the high mountains and arctic regions of Europe. Isolated populations in central Europe and Britain are confined to mountain regions, though a small number of birds have nests at sea-level in the Netherlands.

The nest is a hollow in dwarf vegetation, often unlined. Incubation and care of the young is done by the ♂ who has a duller plumage than the ♀. The species is extraordinarily tame, particularly when nesting. Food is mainly insects and invertebrates.

The species is entirely migratory; European birds winter in North Africa and the Middle East. On spring migration it often forms small parties or 'trips' and stops at traditional sites en route. In winter it is found mainly on muddy shores and lagoons where it feeds on small marine invertebrates.

Migration: Autumn movements mainly August—October with return passage in April—June.

Length:	22 cm
Wing length:	15 cm
Weight:	120 g
Voice:	A soft 'wit-e-wee', also 'prrit' and 'dzwee'
Breeding period:	End of May, July, 1 brood per year. Replacement clutch possible
Size of clutch:	3 (2–4) eggs
Colour of eggs:	Colouring variable from yellow-brown or olive-brown to cinnamon, with dark patches
Size of eggs:	41 × 29 mm
Incubation:	22–26 days, beginning from second egg
Fledging period:	Nidifugous; independent at 4–5 weeks

Chick, Finnish Lapland (Pl)

Steiermark, 30.5.1971 (Li)

eiermark, 17.6.1971 (Li)

ft) ♂ brooding, Steiermark, Austria, 17.6.1971 (Li)

235

Turnstone (Arenaria interpres)

The Turnstone has one of the most northerly breeding ranges of any bird. It breeds on rocky or shingle coasts, offshore islands, grassy islands in the Baltic and in some areas it is found far inland on tundra or other dwarf vegetation.

The nest is a shallow scrape, sometimes lined with plant matter, and on occasions a well-built cup. Incubation is by both sexes, mostly the ♀ at first then increasingly by the ♂. The ♂ takes the major share in rearing the young.

The diet includes all manner of marine invertebrates, crustaceans, molluscs and insects as well as the seed of tundra plants.

The species is mostly migratory, and performs some of the longest migrations in the world, wintering from northern Britain to South Africa. It usually frequents rocky shores or beaches with piles of rotting seaweed, though it will occur on almost any shore, ranging from tropical sandy beaches to muddy lagoons and harbour walls and jetties. Non-breeding birds often summer far south of their breeding range.

Migration: Autumn movements from late July to October, return passage in March–June.

Length:	23 cm
Wing length:	15 cm
Weight:	110 g
Voice:	'Keekekeekekeeke'; when excited 'chuck chuck chuck rurrurrurr'
Breeding period:	Mid-May, June, 1 brood per year. Replacement clutch possible
Size of clutch:	4 (3–5) eggs
Colour of eggs:	Light green to light olive with uneven patches and lines
Size of eggs:	40 × 29 mm
Incubation:	22–23 days, beginning from first egg
Fledging period:	Nidifugous; independent at 4 weeks

n-breeding plumage, Amrum, North Sea, December
$5 (Qu)
t) ♂ brooding, Öland, Sweden, 1973 (Mo)

Non-breeding plumage, Schleswig-Holstein, West Germany (Mö)

Öland, Sweden, 1973 (Mo)

237

Common Snipe (Gallinago gallinago)

The Snipe frequents marshes, damp meadows, bogs and moorland. It is a secretive bird, often difficult to observe. In spring, however, it has a display flight which involves making a drumming noise with the fanned tail-feathers as the bird dives down towards the ground. The nest is usually sited in deep vegetation, a tussock or clump of rushes, and is a hollow lined with grass. Incubation is by the ♀ alone though both parents assist in rearing the young.

The diet is mainly worms, insect larvae, molluscs and other invertebrates which are obtained by probing with the long bill in soft ground.

Northern populations are largely migratory, wintering in western Europe south to Africa. Large numbers may occur in suitable feeding places such as flooded grassland. The species is not normally gregarious, usually rising singly even when numbers are present in the same locality. Small flocks, called 'wisps', are sometimes seen which fly in tight co-ordinated groups like some *calidris* Waders.

Migration: Dispersal from late July with main movements in August— October, return passage in March—April.

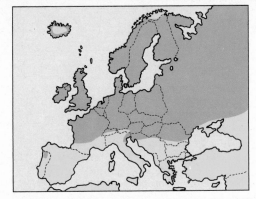

Length:	27 cm
Wing length:	13 cm
Weight:	105 g
Voices:	'Too-ka tyoo-ka'; far-carrying grumbling produced by vibration of tail-feathers. Call 'scaap'
Breeding period:	April, June, 1 brood per year. Replacement clutch and second brood possible
Size of clutch:	4 (3–5) eggs
Colour of eggs:	Greenish to olive-brown, with dark patches and spots
Size of eggs:	39 × 29 mm
Incubation:	18–20 days, from third or fourth egg
Fledging period:	Nidifugous; independent at 5–6 weeks

and, Sweden, 1973 (Mo)

ft) Bavaria, West Germany, early September 1976 (Pf)

Bavaria, May 1977 (Pf)

Young in nest, Amrum, North Sea, June 1973 (Qu)

239

Jack Snipe (Lymnocryptes minimus)

The Jack Snipe is found in the bogs and swamps of the northern coniferous forests and in wet alder or willow woodland. The species has an aerial display similar to the Common Snipe and makes a noise likened to that of a galloping horse. The nest is a shallow cup lined with grass usually on a slight hummock in swampy vegetation. Incubation is by the ♀ alone. The diet is similar to that of the Common Snipe, though the shorter bill means that it cannot probe so deeply in soft ground. It is wholly migratory, wintering in wetland habitats in western and southern Europe as well as in Africa.

The Great Snipe (*Gallinago media*) has a similar distribution though it occurs further south in eastern Europe. It is decreasing in most of its European range perhaps due to habitat change. It inhabits marshy ground often in open woods, birch scrub and wet meadows. It does not have an aerial display but ♂♂ gather to display at leks, usually a raised hummock in marshland. The nest is usually in vegetation, though open sites are used at times. It is a hollow lined with moss or grass and incubation is by the ♀ alone. It is entirely migratory, wintering mostly in tropical Africa.

Migrations: End of March to early May and August to October.

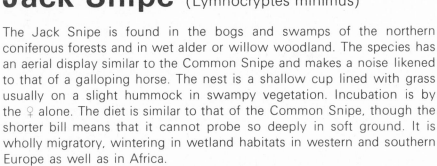

Green = Jack Snipe
Black = Great Snipe

Length:	19 cm	Jack Snipe
Wing length:	11 cm	
Weight:	70 g	
Voice:	Rather silent. In flight 'kitz' or 'kutz'. Courting: drumming noise like Common Snipe	
Breeding period:	Beginning of June, probably 2 broods per year	
Size of clutch:	4 (3) eggs	
Colour of eggs:	Olive-green, with dark brown spots and patches	
Size of eggs:	39 × 27 mm	
Incubation:	18–24 days, beg. from complete clutch	
Fledging period:	Nidifugous; further information unknown	

Length:	28 cm	Great Snipe
Wing length:	14–15 cm	
Weight:	ca 200 g	
Voices:	♂ warbling song; call 'fraank'	
Breeding period:	Beginning of May to beginning of July, 1 brood per year	
Size of clutch:	4 (3) eggs	
Colour of eggs:	Light yellow-grey or grey, sometimes olive with dark olive-brown patches and small dots	
Size of eggs:	45 × 32 mm	
Incubation:	22–24 days	
Fledging period:	Nidifugous; fledged at 3–4 weeks	

...enbach Valley dam, Westerwald, West Germany, 1974 (Be)
Amrum, North Sea, October 1966 (Qu)

Great Snipe ♂ displaying (Gé)

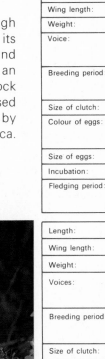

241

Woodcock (Scolopax rusticola)

The Woodcock inhabits forested areas with open rides and good ground-cover of bracken, fallen leaves and other vegetation. The ♂ has a display flight called 'roding' in which it traverses the same route each night, flying with slow, Owl-like wingbeats. The nest is a hollow lined with leaves and other plant matter, usually at the foot of a tree, sometimes hidden in undergrowth. Incubation is by the ♀ only, as is care of the young. The diet is largely earthworms as well as insects and larvae, and some plant matter. The very long bill is used to probe in soft ground.

The northern and eastern populations are migratory, wintering in western and southern Europe, the Middle East and North Africa. British birds are largely resident, though some move as far as Iberia. It is essentially a solitary bird, almost invariably seen singly except when roding, when two or three birds may fly together.

Migration: Autumn movements from mid-September to November, spring passage in March–April.

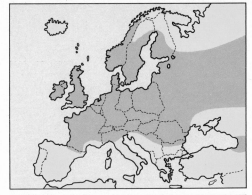

Length:	34 cm
Wing length:	20 cm
Weight:	340 g
Voice:	During roding flight deep 'quorr', followed by a sharp 'tsiwik'
Breeding period:	Mid-March, July, 1–2 broods per year
Size of clutch:	4 (3–5) eggs
Colour of eggs:	Cream to reddish brown with small spots and larger patches
Size of eggs:	43 × 34 mm
Incubation:	20–23 days, beg. from complete clutch
Fledging period:	Nidifugous; able to fly from 15 days, independent at 6 weeks

um, North Sea, October 1971 (Qu)

Chick, Marburg, West Germany, May (Tö)

Tyrol, 12.6.1967 (Wi)

Bavaria, West Germany, September 1977 (Zei)

Curlew (Numenius arquata)

The Curlew inhabits moorland, heaths, marshes and agricultural land. These areas echo to its bubbling, melodious song in spring. The nest is a hollow lined with grass or other plant material, usually sited in low vegetation such as heather or grasses. Incubation is by both sexes, though mainly the ♀. The young are tended by both parents at first, but later only by the ♂. The diet consists of insects, larvae, worms, seeds and berries.

The northern and eastern populations are migratory, wintering in western and southern Europe, parts of the Middle East and Africa. In winter it is found on muddy shorelines, estuaries and salt-marshes as well as wet agricultural land. It probes deep into mud to find molluscs and marine invertebrates. It is markedly gregarious outside the breeding season, occurring in large flocks on migration and in winter.

Migration: Autumn passage from mid-July to October, returning in March–April.

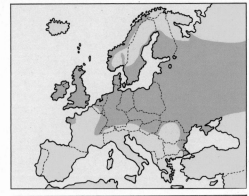

Length:	55 cm
Wing length:	30 cm
Weight:	800 g
Voice:	'Coorlee-coorlee'. Courtship: bubbling trill
Breeding period:	Mid-April to May, 1 brood per year. Replacement clutch possible
Size of clutch:	4 (3–5) eggs
Colour of eggs:	Light green to olive-brown, with dark patches
Size of eggs:	67 × 47 mm
Incubation:	26–30 days, beg. from complete clutch
Fledging period:	Nidifugous; independent at 5–6 weeks

...ria, June 1972 (Pf)

Bavaria, West Germany, 1956 (Li)

Chick, Lower Saxony, West Germany (We)

Bavaria, 23.4.1974 (Pf)

245

Whimbrel (Numenius phaeopus)

The Whimbrel tends to favour more upland or northerly habitats to those of the Curlew. It nests in more open areas such as tundra, and frequents drier areas than the Curlew. The nest is a hollow lined with a little moss, lichen or other plant material. It is often sited near to a rock or stump where the off-duty bird may keep watch. Both parents share in incubation and in rearing the young. The diet is similar to that of the Curlew but obtains less food by probing, and more by pecking from the surface or in low vegetation.

The Whimbrel is entirely migratory, wintering in south-west Iberia, North Africa and the Middle East and the coasts of tropical Africa. Occasionally a few birds may overwinter in northern Europe. In winter it occurs more frequently on rocky shores than the Curlew and is less gregarious, though small flocks occur regularly.

In Britain the Whimbrel breeds only in the Northern Isles.

Migration: Autumn passage from mid-July to October, return in spring from April to June.

Length:	40 cm
Wing length:	25 cm
Weight:	350 g
Voice:	Call, 'titti-titti-titti-titti-titti-tit'; also bubbling song similar to that of Curlew
Breeding period:	Mid-May, end of June, 1 brood per year. Replacement clutch possible
Size of clutch:	4 (3–5) eggs
Colour of eggs:	Olive-green to brownish, with dark brown spots and patches
Size of eggs:	58 × 42 mm
Incubation:	24–28 days, beg. from complete clutch
Fledging period:	Nidifugous; able to fly at 4–5 weeks

entral Sweden, 1.7.1968 (Sy)

Juv., Central Sweden, 16.6.1968 (Sy)

Central Sweden, 30.6.1968 (Sy)

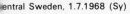

eft) Ad. with chicks, Central Sweden, 10.7.1968 (Sy)

247

Black-tailed Godwit (Limosa limosa)

The Black-tailed Godwit nests in grassy meadows, marshland, bogs and rough pasture in north central Europe. A separate race breeds in Iceland. It is territorial in the breeding season and will drive off intruders. It has a noisy call, particularly in aerial display. The nest is usually in lush vegetation and is a hollow lined with grass. Incubation is by both sexes who also share in the care of the young. It feeds on a variety of invertebrates, including worms, insects and molluscs, probing in the mud with its long bill, and also picking food from stems of grasses and other plants.

The species is migratory: Icelandic birds winter in Ireland and south-west Britain. The main population winters in south-west and south-east Europe, North Africa and parts of tropical Africa. Smaller numbers also winter in Britain and parts of western Europe. Outside the breeding season it is gregarious and frequents saltmarshes, muddy estuaries and the shores of rivers and lakes.

Migration: Autumn movements from late July to September, spring passage mainly mid-March to early May.

The species formerly bred in Britain but became extinct in the 1830s. From the 1950s small numbers have colonised parts of East Anglia and elsewhere. A few pairs, probably of the Icelandic race, nest in the Northern Isles.

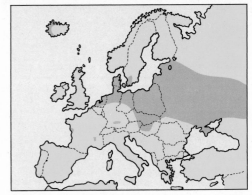

Length:	41 cm
Wing length:	21 cm
Weight:	250 g
Voice:	'Wicka-wicka'. Courtship: 'wotta-we-do'
Breeding period:	End of April, June, 1 brood per year. Replacement clutch possible
Size of clutch:	4 (3–5) eggs
Colour of eggs:	Light-green to olive-brown, with few or many dark spots
Size of eggs:	55 × 38 mm
Incubation:	22–24 days, from third or fourth egg
Fledging period:	Nidifugous; able to fly at 4 weeks

ewinkel, June 1969 (Li)

ft) Seewinkel, Austria, 1961 (Li)

Seewinkel, 1959 (Li)

Bavaria, West Germany, 28.4.1968 (Li)

249

Green Sandpiper (Tringa ochropus)

The Green Sandpiper frequents swampy woodland or forested areas near open water in the north and east of Europe. It nests in trees, usually conifers, using the old nests of other birds, particularly thrushes and Woodpigeon. It may add some lining material of moss or lichen but does not repair the nests structurally. Occasionally it will nest in the top of a hollow stump or even on the ground. Incubation is by both sexes, mainly the ♀, and both parents share in rearing the young which jump from the nest after a few hours. Food is mainly aquatic insects and other invertebrates and is obtained along the edges of streams and pools as well as in marshy ground.

The species is entirely migratory, wintering in small numbers in western Europe, including Britain, but mostly in Mediterranean countries southwards into Africa. It is not gregarious, and when on passage or wintering is rarely seen in the company of others. It frequents streams, small pools, sewage farms and marshland in winter, and on passage it prefers vegetated banks to open areas rarely being seen on the open shore.

Migration: Autumn passage from June to November, with return in March—May.

Length:	23 cm
Wing length:	14 cm
Weight:	80 g
Voice:	Taking off: 'twee' or 'twee-weet-weet'. Courting: 'chee-tyoo-tee'
Breeding period:	Mid-April, June, 1 brood per year. Replacement clutch possible
Size of clutch:	4 (2—3) eggs
Colour of eggs:	Cream, with olive or green tint and brownish flecks
Size of eggs:	39 × 28 mm
Incubation:	20—23 days, beg. from complete clutch
Fledging period:	Nidifugous; independent at ca 4 weeks

haning Reservoir, Bavaria, Sept. 1976 (Kü)

*t) Bavaria, West Germany, 15.8.1976 (Li)

Clutch in an old Blackbird's nest, Südholstein, West Germany, 28.4.1972 (Ki)

251

Wood Sandpiper (Tringa glareola)

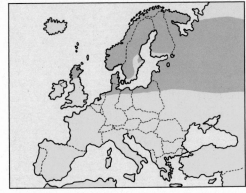

The Wood Sandpiper has a similar distribution to that of the Green Sandpiper but it breeds further north and prefers more open, less wooded areas. The nest is usually on the ground in a tussock or other raised patch. It is a scrape lined with grass and leaves. Sometimes the old nest of a thrush or other bird is used in trees or bushes. Incubation is by both sexes, though the ♀ takes the larger share. Both parents share in rearing the young at first; later only the ♂ has this responsibility. Food consists mainly of aquatic insects, worms and molluscs.

The species is entirely migratory, European birds wintering mainly in Africa, both tropical and sub-tropical. It is more gregarious than the Green Sandpiper and often occurs in small flocks on migration. It is rarely seen on the open shore, preferring muddy borders of lakes, pools and rivers, marshland and other wetland areas.

A small population breed in Britain, mainly in the Highlands of Scotland, where it is very rare.

Migration: Autumn movements from July to September, returning in April to early June.

Length:	20 cm
Wing length:	12 cm
Weight:	70 g
Voice:	'Giff-giff-giff'. Courting: 'twee-twee-twee', resembling song of Woodlark
Breeding period:	Beginning of May, June, 1 brood per year. Replacement clutch possible
Size of clutch:	4 (3) eggs
Colour of eggs:	Light green to light olive, with brown patches
Size of eggs:	38 × 27 mm
Incubation:	22–23 days, beg. from complete clutch
Fledging period:	Nidifugous; independent at 4 weeks

aria, 29.8.1974 (Pf)

) Bavaria, West Germany, 5.9.1976 (Pf)

Chicks (Ki)

Wood Sandpiper's eggs (Ki)

Redshank (Tringa totanus)

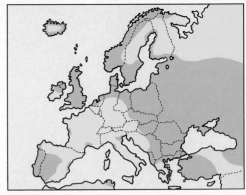

The Redshank is an inhabitant of grassy marshland, wet meadows, salt-marshes and swampy heathland. It has become scarce in much of continental Europe away from the coast due to drainage of wetland. It is a noisy, restless bird and is conspicuous in its breeding areas, often perching on fence posts. The nest is a hollow lined with grass or other plant material, usually well concealed in a grass tussock. Incubation is by both sexes as is the care of the young.

The Redshank feeds on a variety of insects, aquatic creatures and plant matter including seeds and berries. It obtains food by picking amongst marshy vegetation as well as by wading in shallow water.

The species is largely migratory, northern and eastern birds moving furthest. It winters in western Europe, the Mediterranean, the Middle East and as far as South Africa. It is mainly coastal in winter, favouring estuaries and muddy shores, where it probes for molluscs and marine invertebrates with its long bill. It is gregarious outside the breeding season and occurs in large flocks.

Migration: Autumn passage from July to October, returning in March–May.

Length:	28 cm
Wing length:	16 cm
Weight:	130 g
Voice:	Melodious 'tyoo-too-too'. Courtship an oft-repeated 'tyo-odle-tyo-odle'
Breeding period:	Mid-April, June, 1 brood per year. Replacement clutch possible
Size of clutch:	4 (3–5) eggs
Colour of eggs:	Yellowish to rusty brown, with dark flecks, increasing towards the larger end
Size of eggs:	45 × 31 mm
Incubation:	22–24 days, beg. from complete clutch
Fledging period:	Nidifugous; independent at 4–5 weeks

(*ft and above*) Öland, Sweden, 1973 (Mo)

Chicks, Shetland, June 1976 (Ma)

Anatolia, Turkey, 14.5.1975 (Li)

Spotted Redshank (Tringa erythropus)

The Spotted Redshank has a northerly distribution frequenting open areas near the treeline. These may be swampy or dry places ranging from woodland clearings to shrub tundra.

The nest is a shallow scrape among low vegetation, sometimes lined with moss or lichen. It is often near a stone, branch or similar marker. Incubation is mainly by the ♂ who also cares for the young, though both parents may do so at first.

It feeds on aquatic insects, small fish, crustaceans and other invertebrates. It will wade in deep water and even swim with head and neck submerged. It is entirely migratory, wintering in small numbers in western Europe and in Africa but mainly in the Mediterranean countries. It is gregarious outside the breeding season, when it occurs in small parties which often feed communally. It favours muddy shorelines, salt-marshes and shallow margins of lakes, and freely associates with the Redshank and the Greenshank.

Migration: Autumn dispersal from mid-June with main passage in August–October. Spring passage in April–May.

Length:	30 cm
Wing length:	17 cm
Weight:	180 g
Voice:	'Tchu-it', or a scolding 'tick-tick'
Breeding period:	End of May, June, 1 brood per year
Size of clutch:	4 (3) eggs
Colour of eggs:	Light to olive-green, with marked spotting; spots increase at larger end
Size of eggs:	47 × 32 mm
Incubation:	22–25 days, beg. from complete clutch
Fledging period:	Nidifugous; independent at 4–5 weeks

eding plumage, Finnish Lapland, June 1970 (Willy)

't) Non-breeding plumage, Bavaria, West Germany, 14.4.1976 (Li)

Immature plumage, Bavaria, 20.8.1968 (Li)

Clutch near a stick as 'marker', Lapland, June 1970 (Willy)

Greenshank (Tringa nebularia)

The Greenshank inhabits open moorland, tundra, swampy clearings in birch and coniferous woods and margins of lakes. It is often found in areas with dead or decaying vegetation.

The nest is a hollow lined with available plant matter and usually sited near a tree stump, rock or dead branch. Incubation is by both sexes, but mainly the ♀. Both parents share in rearing the young. It feeds on insects, crustaceans, aquatic invertebrates and to a lesser extent on small fish. The food is often obtained by wading in quite deep water and making sweeping movements with the partly open bill.

The species is entirely migratory, wintering in small numbers in western Europe, but mainly in the Mediterranean countries, the Middle East and Africa. It is found on muddy lagoons, river margins, pools and marshes, and rarely on open shores.

Migration: Autumn passage from July to October, returning in April—May.

Length:	30 cm
Wing length:	19 cm
Weight:	180 g
Voice:	Melodious 'chu-chu-chu'; song, a rich 'ru-tu-ru-tu...'
Breeding period:	May, June, 1 brood per year. Replacement clutch possible
Size of clutch:	4 (3–5) eggs
Colour of eggs:	Dirty white to yellowish-brown, irregularly flecked with dark patches and scrawls
Size of eggs:	51 × 35 mm
Incubation:	24–25 days, beg. from complete clutch
Fledging period:	Nidifugous; independent at 4–5 weeks

land, 21.6.1972 (Sy)

Bavaria, April 1959 (Pf)

Lapland, 20.6.1972 (Sy)

t) Bavaria, West Germany, 10.9.1973 (Pf)

259

Common Sandpiper

(Actitis hypoleucos)

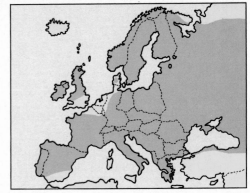

The Common Sandpiper frequents the margins of clear lakes and pools, fast-flowing streams and rivers in both open and wooded country. In the south of its range it also frequents slow-moving rivers with large sand or shingle banks. The nest is a shallow scrape lined with plant material or flood debris, usually in low vegetation or in the shelter of small bush above the flood-level. Incubation and rearing the young is shared by both parents. The diet includes aquatic insects, molluscs, crustaceans and a small amount of seeds and other plant matter. It feeds along the water's edge, often perching on rocks or branches in shallow water. The species is largely migratory except in the southernmost part of the range. It winters mainly in tropical Africa, though small numbers occur regularly in western Europe, the Mediterranean and Middle East countries. It is not markedly gregarious and usually occurs singly or in small parties. It frequents a variety of habitats in winter from inland waters to mangrove swamps and even rocky shores or jetties. It is rarely found on mudflats or open shores.

Migration: Autumn movements from July to October returning in late March to May.

Length:	19 cm
Wing length:	11 cm
Weight:	50 g
Voice:	Shrill whistling 'hee-dee-dee'. Song, a longer series 'heedeeedeedeedee'
Breeding period:	May, June, 1 brood per year. Replacement clutch possible
Size of clutch:	4 (3–5) eggs
Colour of eggs:	Yellow-brown to reddish, with dark flecks
Size of eggs:	36 × 26 mm
Incubation:	21–23 days, beg. from complete clutch
Fledging period:	Nidifugous; able to fly well at 15 days, independent at 4 weeks

n., Bavaria, 31.8.1976 (Pf)

Chicks, Finnish Lapland (Pl)

Bavaria, 12.5.1974 (Pf)

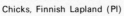

♂) Bavaria, West Germany, 30.5.1977 (Li)

261

Purple Sandpiper (Calidris maritima)

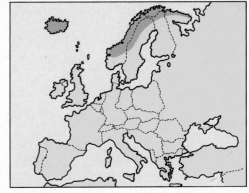

The Purple Sandpiper has a northerly distribution and breeds on swampy areas of tundra, mountain tops, shingle ridges and offshore islands. The nest is a deep scrape lined with lichen or moss and made by the ♂. Incubation is by both sexes but chiefly the ♂, who also rears the young. The food is a variety of insects, spiders, seeds and other plant material. In winter it is almost entirely coastal, frequenting ice-free coasts in the breeding range, the more northerly breeding birds migrating to western Europe. It is usually found on rocky shores or shingle where it searches for marine invertebrates, crustaceans and molluscs among rotting seaweed or at the water's edge. It is gregarious, and usually occurs in small flocks, commonly associating with the Turnstone. Small numbers of non-breeders summer south of the breeding range.

Migration: Northerly populations move from July to November, returning in April—May.

Length:	21 cm
Wing length:	13 cm
Weight:	70 g
Voice:	Disyllabic 'weet-wit', also trilling courtship song, rather silent in winter
Breeding period:	Mid-May, mid-June, 1 brood per year. Replacement clutch possible
Size of clutch:	4 (3) eggs
Colour of eggs:	Pale olive-green, blotched and speckled dark brown or purplish-grey
Size of eggs:	38 × 27 mm
Incubation:	21—22 days, beginning from last egg
Fledging period:	Nidifugous; independent at *ca* 3—4 weeks

…eden (Pl)

) Non-breeding plumage, Cuxhaven, Holland, 26.2.1973 (Bö)

Sweden (Pl)

263

Little Stint (Calidris minuta)

The Little Stint breeds only in the extreme north of Europe, frequenting tundra in low-lying coastal or riverine areas. The nest is a tiny cup lined with moss or lichen sometimes in the shelter of a low plant. Incubation and care of the young is shared by both parents but the ♂ takes the larger part. It is often extraordinarily tame and trusting on the breeding grounds. The diet is mostly small insects and their larvae, particularly mosquitoes.

The species is entirely migratory, wintering in the Mediterranean countries, the Middle East and Africa as far south as the Cape. It is gregarious outside the breeding season, occurring in large flocks. It favours sandy or muddy shore, shallow pools, saltpans and inland waters. In winter it feeds mostly on small aquatic invertebrates such as crustaceans and molluscs.

Migration: Autumn movements from July to October, returning in April–June.

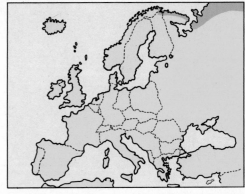

Length:	13 cm
Wing length:	9.5 cm
Weight:	30 g
Voice:	Whirring 'tirrrit-tit-tit'
Breeding period:	End of June, July, 1, possibly 2 broods
Size of clutch:	4 (3) eggs
Colour of eggs:	Whitish to light olive with small spots and patches
Size of eggs:	29 × 21 mm
Incubation:	Unknown
Fledging period:	Unknown

rum, North Sea, August 1965 (Qu)

t) Ad., Bavaria, West Germany, 16.9.1969 (Li)

Imm., Bavaria, 12.9.1969 (Li)

265

Temminck's Stint

(Calidris temminckii)

The range of the Temminck's Stint extends further south than that of the Little Stint. It nests in shrub tundra and boggy ground especially in river valleys or borders of lakes and pools. The nest is a shallow scrape lined with moss, lichen or other plant material. Incubation is by both sexes but chiefly the ♂. Both parents tend the chicks at first but later this is done by the ♂ alone. When double-brooded the ♀ may sit on another clutch while the ♂ incubates the first. The food is mainly insects and larvae and a small amount of plant material. The species is entirely migratory, wintering in parts of the Middle East but chiefly in tropical Africa; more eastern breeding birds migrate to southern Asia. In winter it frequents inland lakes and pools with muddy shores, rarely visiting the coast. It is not gregarious though small parties may be seen on migration. Like the Little Stint, it is often tame and trusting, especially on the breeding grounds.

Migration: Mid-July to September in autumn, returning in late April to early June.

Length:	14 cm
Wing length:	9.5 cm
Weight:	30 g
Voice:	Short whirring 'tirr', and 'trrreee' like Skylark
Breeding period:	Mid-June–July; may have two broods, each incubated by one of the pair
Size of clutch:	4 (3) eggs
Colour of eggs:	Light brown to grey-green with dark patches
Size of eggs:	28 × 20 mm
Incubation:	19–22 days, beg. from complete clutch
Fledging period:	Nidifugous; independent at 3 weeks

. breeding plumage, Finnish Lapland (Pl)

ft) ♀ brooding, Lapland, 24.6.1972 (Sy)

Imm. plumage, Bavaria, West Germany, August 1967 (Li)

Lapland, 24.6.1972 (Sy)

267

Dunlin (Calidris alpina)

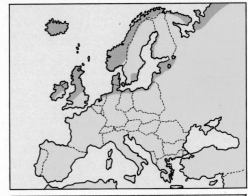

The Dunlin is predominantly a bird of the arctic tundra but one of the races (*C.a. shinzii*) breeds in Britain and parts of continental Europe. It is found on moorland, lowland peat-mosses, rough grassland and, in some areas, saltmarshes. The nest is a small hollow, usually in a tussock of grass and lined with dry grass or leaves. Incubation is by both sexes as is the care of the young, though this is left to the ♀ in the later stages. The diet consists mainly of insects and larvae with very little plant material. The species is migratory, wintering from Britain and parts of Scandinavia to the Mediterranean and North Africa, depending upon the race involved.

It is gregarious outside the breeding season and is often found in vast flocks. It winters on almost all types of coast except rocky shores, but shows a preference for wide mudflats and tidal estuaries. In winter it feeds on marine invertebrates, crustaceans, small molluscs and insects.

Migration: Mainly late July to November, returning in March—May.

Length:	18 cm, varies according to race
Wing length:	11 cm, ditto
Weight:	40 g, ditto
Voice:	A weak 'dzeep' or 'terrp'. Song is a rich trill uttered in display
Breeding period:	End of April, June, 1 brood per year, exceptionally 2 broods. Replacement clutch possible
Size of clutch:	4 (3–5) eggs
Colour of eggs:	Yellowish brown, olive-brown or reddish brown. Very variable dark patches
Size of eggs:	35 × 25 mm
Incubation:	21–22 days, beg. from complete clutch
Fledging period:	Nidifugous; independent at 3 weeks

♀, Öland, Sweden, June 1970 (Di)

Chick, Öland, May 1973 (Pa)

Öland, June 1970 (Di)

*t) Echinger Reservoir, Bavaria, West Germany, April 1978 (Pf)

Ruff (Philomachus pugnax)

The Ruff breeds in low-lying marshy areas, damp meadows and, in the north, tundra with low vegetation. ♂♂ have a distinctive breeding plumage and are promiscuous. They have a communal display or lek usually in an open grassy area where the ♂♂ posture and sometimes fight while the ♀♀ look on. The nest is a hollow lined with dry grass, usually concealed in tall grass except in tundra areas. Incubation and care of the young are carried out by the ♀ alone. The diet includes insects, worms, molluscs and perhaps some seeds.

The species is migratory, wintering from western Europe, south through Mediterranean countries to tropical Africa. It is not particularly gregarious, though it occurs in small flocks in winter and sometimes in large numbers on passage. It winters on muddy shores of pools, lakes and lagoons as well as on estuaries and mudflats.

Migration: July—November in autumn, returning in late February to May.

Length:	♂ 30 cm, ♀ 23 cm
Wing length:	♂ 19 cm, ♀ 16 cm
Weight:	♂ 190 g, ♀ 125 g
Voice:	Rarely heard, sometimes 'tu-whit' or 'kuk-kuk-kuk'
Breeding period:	End of April, end of June, 1 brood per year. Replacement clutch possible
Size of clutch:	4 (3) eggs
Colour of eggs:	Light to olive-green, with dark patches and spots
Size of eggs:	44 × 31 mm
Incubation:	20—21 days, beg. from complete clutch
Fledging period:	Nidifugous; independent at 4 weeks

m., Bavaria, West Germany, 1.9.1977 (Pf)

eft) ♂♂ at lek, Jämtland, Sweden, June 1975 (Zi)

Chick, Finnish Lapland, June 1976 (Willy)

Handöl, Sweden, July 1976 (Di)

271

Avocet (Recurvirostra avosetta)

The Avocet is found on brackish lagoons, shallow salt water and alkaline lakes where mud or sandbanks provide a suitable nesting site. It breeds in colonies sometimes in association with gulls or terns. The nest is a scrape on open mud or sand, sometimes lined with a little plant material. Incubation and care of the young is shared by both parents. The diet includes small crustaceans, molluscs, insects and fish-spawn. It usually feeds by wading in shallow water and making sweeping movements of the upturned bill, and it will also swim in deeper water.

The northern population is migratory, wintering in southern Europe, Noth Africa and the Middle East. Large numbers winter in the Rift Valley of Africa, but it is not known if they include European birds. A few winter in Britain and north-west Europe.

The northern population has increased in recent years and the species re-colonised Britain in the late 1940s after being exterminated.

Migration: Late July—October, returning in early March—May.

Length:	44 cm
Wing length:	22 cm
Weight:	350 g
Voice:	Fluting 'klooit'; when excited, 'clickit-clickit'
Breeding period:	End of April, June, 1 brood per year. Replacement clutch possible
Size of clutch:	4 (3–5) eggs
Colour of eggs:	Variable, clay-coloured with small dark spots and patches
Size of eggs:	50 × 35 mm
Incubation:	22–24 days, beg. from complete clutch
Fledging period:	Nidifugous; independent at 6 weeks

., Seewinkel, Austria, 1961 (Li)

Seewinkel, 1961 (Li)

Northern Greece, 19.5.1972 (Li)

-ft) Ad. with young, Central Anatolia, Turkey, 1.6.1974 (Pf)

273

Black-winged Stilt

(Himantopus himantopus)

The Black-winged Stilt frequents shallow lagoons, the margins of fresh-water or brackish pools, mudflats and ricefields. It breeds in loose colonies and the nests are shallow scrapes with little or no lining material in dry sites or are built up with mud or sited in a tussock. Incubation and care of the young is shared by both parents. The diet consists mainly of insects and larvae, small crustaceans, molluscs and small fish; the unusually long legs enable the Stilt to feed in deeper water than most species.

Black-winged Stilts are partially migratory, birds from the northern and more easterly parts of the range moving furthest. In winter it is found in Mediterranean and North-African countries; some possibly move to tropical Africa.

Migration: Mainly September—October in autumn with return passage in April to early May.

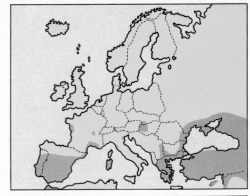

Length:	38 cm
Wing length:	24 cm
Weight:	160 g
Voice:	Yelping 'kyip-kyip-kyip'
Breeding period:	End of April, beginning of June, 1 brood per year. Replacement clutch possible
Size of clutch:	4 (3–5) eggs
Colour of eggs:	Clay-brown with small dark spots and patches
Size of eggs:	44 × 31 mm
Incubation:	25–26 days, beg. from complete clutch
Fledging period:	Nidifugous; independent at 4 weeks

cedonia, Greece, 25.5.1969 (Sy)

Seewinkel, Austria, June 1965 (Li)

♀ turning eggs, Central Anatolia, 12.6.1974 (Pf)

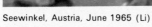

⟨) Ad. ♂, Central Anatolia, Turkey, 8.6.1974 (Pf)

275

Red-necked Phalarope

(Phalaropus lobatus)

The Red-necked Phalarope inhabits fresh-water pools, the margins of lakes and low islands in rivers or offshore. A good growth of emergent vegetation such as grasses and other marsh-plants is essential. The nest is sited in a tussock of vegetation close to the water, and is a hollow lined with grass or other plant material. Incubation and care of the young is by the ♂ alone, which is slightly duller in plumage than the ♀. The food, which is mainly insects and aquatic larvae and small crustaceans, is obtained from the surface of the water whilst swimming as well as from dry land. It has a method of spinning on the water to form a small whirl-pool which sucks insects into its centre.

The species is entirely migratory, wintering off the coasts of Arabia and West Africa, though distribution of European birds in winter is not adequately known. The diet in winter is probably animal plankton taken from the surface of the ocean.

Migration: Departs breeding areas in late July to August, returning in May or June. On passage it may occur on fresh or salt water and is often very tame and trusting.

Length:	18 cm
Wing length:	11 cm
Weight:	40 g
Voice:	Shrill 'ch-ritt' or 'pritt'
Breeding period:	End of May, end of June, 1 brood per year. Replacement clutch possible
Size of clutch:	4 (3) eggs
Colour of eggs:	Greenish to olive-brown with irregular black-brown spots
Size of eggs:	30 × 21 mm
Incubation:	18–20 days, beg. from complete clutch
Fledging period:	Nidifugous; independent at *ca* 3 weeks

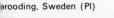

brooding, Sweden (Pl)

Chick, Central Norway, 26.6.1968 (Sy)

Handöl, Sweden, July 1976 (Di)

t) ♀ in breeding plumage, Sweden (Pl)

277

Stone Curlew (Burhinus oedicnemus)

The Stone Curlew frequents steppe and semi-desert country, dry arable land, open dry heath and areas of shingle or dry mud near rivers or lakes. The nest is a scrape on bare ground sometimes sparsely lined with pebbles or plant debris. Incubation and care of the young is shared by both sexes. The diet includes large insects such as grasshoppers, small reptiles, worms and occasionally small mammals or nestling birds. It is a rather secretive bird and feeds mostly at night.

In the south of its range it is mainly resident but northern and eastern birds winter in the Mediterranean and North-African countries and parts of the Middle East. It is often seen in small flocks, even in the breeding season, and in autumn may occur in quite large numbers.

Migration: Northern populations move out in August–October, returning in March and April.

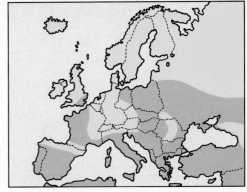

Length:	40 cm
Wing length:	24 cm
Weight:	400 g
Voice:	Melodious, far-carrying calls 'kee-rr-eel' or 'cour-lee'
Breeding period:	April, June, 1–2 broods per year. Replacement clutch possible
Size of clutch:	2 (3) eggs
Colour of eggs:	Sandy, with dark patches and scrawls
Size of eggs:	54 × 38 mm
Incubation:	25–27 days, beg. from second egg
Fledging period:	Nidifugous; able to fly at 4 weeks, independent at 8 weeks

ntral Anatolia, 25.5.1974 (Pf)

ft) Repelling a tortoise from the nest, Anatolia, Turkey, 8.5.1975 (Li)

Young, not yet fledged, Macedonia, Yugoslavia, 1969 (Li)

Anatolia, 28.5.1974 (Li)

Collared Pratincole

(Glareola pratincola)

The Collared Pratincole inhabits open areas of dry mud near water, sparse grasslands, dry steppe and fallow arable land.

It is a sociable bird and breeds in loose colonies of up to several hundred pairs. These colonies depend upon suitable areas for nesting and feeding and may change considerably accordingly. The eggs are laid in a natural hollow, often a hoofprint, or in patches of sparse vegetation and sometimes even on dry cowpats. Incubation is by both sexes as is the care of the young. The food is mainly large insects taken on the ground and in the air. Flocks will feed together in a Tern-like manner where food is abundant. It destroys large numbers of insects which are harmful to agriculture.

The species is entirely migratory, wintering, often in very large flocks, in the African savanna as far as South Africa.

Migration: Late August to early October, returning in April and early May.

Length:	25 cm
Wing length:	19 cm
Weight:	50 g
Voice:	Tern-like 'tree' or 'kikki-kirrik'
Breeding period:	End of April, June, 1 brood per year. Replacement clutch possible
Size of clutch:	3 (2–4) eggs
Colour of eggs:	Sandy or greenish with large dark spots and patches
Size of eggs:	33 × 24 mm
Incubation:	17–18 days, beg. from complete clutch
Fledging period:	Nidicolous; able to fly at 3 weeks, independent at 4 weeks

Northern Greece, 18.5.1972 (Li)

(left) Macedonia, Greece, 27.5.1977 (Pf)

Northern Greece, 23.5.1972 (Li)

Northern Greece, 23.5.1972 (Li)

281

Arctic Skua (Stercorarius parasiticus)

The Arctic Skua is found on coastal moorland, tundra and offshore islands. It is very territorial and will drive intruders away from the nest whether avian or human, dive-bombing to the point of striking. It also has a convincing manner of injury-feigning. It nests in loose colonies, though pairs have strict territories within the colony. The nest is a shallow depression sometimes lined with a little dry grass or other plant material. Incubation is by both sexes as is the care of the young. There are several colour-morphs which freely interbreed, the pale birds being more frequent in the north of the range. The food is mostly fish, much of it obtained by robbing Kittiwakes and Terns of their catch (kleptoparasitism); it will also take insects, carrion and small mammals.

It is a long-range migrant, spending the winter entirely at sea off the coasts of Brazil and Angola north to North Africa.

Migration: Leave breeding colonies in August—September, returning in late April to June.

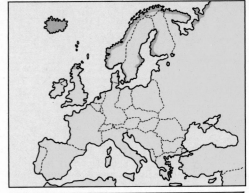

Length:	46 cm
Wing length:	32 cm
Weight:	300 g
Voice:	A loud wailing 'ka-aaow'
Breeding period:	End of May, June, 1 brood per year. Replacement clutch possible
Size of clutch:	2 (1) eggs
Colour of eggs:	Olive-brown, with dark spots and patches
Size of eggs:	57 × 40 mm
Incubation:	24—28 days, beginning from first egg
Fledging period:	Nidicolous; leaving the nest after a few days, but remaining nearby. Independent at 7 weeks

Chick in nest, Foula, June 1973 (Zi)

Norway (Pl)

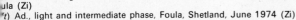

...tic Skua chasing a Great Skua from its territory, ...ula (Zi)

...t) Ad., light and intermediate phase, Foula, Shetland, June 1974 (Zi)

283

Great Skua (Stercorarius skua)

The Great Skua is found on moorland, rough pasture, grassy islands and hills. It is strongly territorial and aggressive towards intruders, often striking other birds and humans. It is not strictly colonial but nests in proximity to others. The nest is a shallow depression usually lined with dry grass. Incubation is by both sexes as is care of the young.

The diet is varied, ranging from eggs and nestlings to full-grown birds up to the size of Herring Gull, fish, often robbed from other seabirds, carrion, offal and small mammals. It will follow fishing boats, taking discarded fish from the surface or robbing gulls of their catch.

It is entirely migratory, pelagic in winter ranging from the Atlantic coast of Iberia to the Caribbean. Small numbers also enter the Mediterranean or remain in northern waters.

Migration: Dispersal from breeding colonies in September–October returning in late March–May.

The Pomarine Skua (*Stercorarius pomarinus*) breeds in the high arctic and is a passage migrant in western Europe (see below).

Length:	58 cm
Wing length:	41 cm
Weight:	1500 g
Voice:	'Whaa-whaa-whaa', and a deep 'tuk . . .tuk'
Breeding period:	Mid-May, June, 1 brood per year. Replacement clutch possible
Size of clutch:	2 (1) eggs
Colour of eggs:	Brown to olive-green, with a few dark or light brown patches
Size of eggs:	70 × 49 mm
Incubation:	28–30 days
Fledging period:	Nidicolous; independent at 6–7 weeks

ula, June 1972

Young Pomarine Skua (*S. pomarinus*), Forggensee, Füssen, West Germany, 4.10.1966 (Wi)

Shetland, June 1976 (Ma)

ft) Ad., Foula, Shetland, June 1972 (Zi)

285

Long-tailed Skua

(Stercorarius longicaudus)

The Long-tailed Skua breeds on high open moorland and tundra; it is not particularly coastal and will breed far inland. Its breeding distribution and numbers vary considerably with the availability of its main prey, lemmings, which have cycles of abundance. It nests in very loose colonies, the nest being a shallow depression sometimes lined with a little dry plant material. Incubation is by both sexes as is the care of the young. Though active in defence of the territory it rarely strikes intruders and is not as aggressive as the Arctic Skua. It feeds mainly on small mammals, particularly lemmings, also insects, crustaceans and berries. The species has a graceful, buoyant flight and frequently hovers when searching for prey.

It is migratory, probably wintering in the southern Atlantic, but its exact winter quarters are not fully known. It is completely pelagic at this season and probably feeds on small fish and surface plankton.

Migration: Leaves breeding areas in August—October, returning in May and early June.

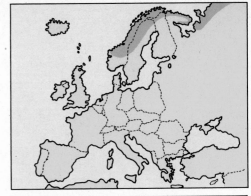

Length:	53 cm, including long tail streamers
Wing length:	31 cm
Weight:	200 g
Voice:	Falcon-like 'kreeeh'
Breeding period:	June, beginning of July. Replacement clutch possible
Size of clutch:	2 eggs
Colour of eggs:	Greenish to olive-brown with sparse dark brown or dark grey flecks at the larger end
Size of eggs:	55 × 38 mm
Incubation:	23 days
Fledging period:	Nidicolous; the young can leave the nest at a few days and are able to fly at *ca* 3 weeks

nish Lapland, July 1969 (Willy)

t) Ad. (Ge)

Finnish Lapland, July 1969 (Schu)

Great Black-backed Gull

(Larus marinus)

The Great Black-backed Gull breeds on seacliffs, on islands and flat-topped stacks, and on moorland or mosses sometimes quite far from the sea. The nest is a pile of grass, seaweed, heather or other plant matter and is built by both sexes. Incubation and care of the young is also shared by the parents. It may nest colonially or in single pairs.

The diet is varied, mostly fish, eggs and young of other birds, full-grown birds such as auks and shearwaters, all manner of carrion and edible debris thrown up by the sea. It will follow fishing boats to take discarded fish and offal and also rob other birds of food.

The species is partially migratory, northern populations moving furthest. It winters on the coasts of western Europe and is showing an increasing tendency to occur inland, feeding at rubbish tips and roosting on reservoirs or lakes. It freely associates with other large gulls and will form large flocks.

Migration: Autumn movements mainly September—November, returning in March—May.

Length:	64—79 cm
Wing length:	48—51 cm
Weight:	1700 g
Voice:	Deep harsh 'ouk' or series of calls, 'uk-uk-uk'
Breeding period:	Mid-April, May, 1 brood per year. Replacement clutch possible
Size of clutch:	2—3 eggs
Colour of eggs:	Variable sandy, light olive or rusty brown, with dark spots and patches
Size of eggs:	77 × 54 mm
Incubation:	26—30 days, beginning before final egg
Fledging period:	Nidicolous; able to fly at ca 8 weeks

...ula, Shetland (Zi)

...t) Shetland, June 1976

Chick, Foula, May 1974 (Zi)

Shetland, June 1976 (Ma)

Lesser Black-backed Gull

(Larus fuscus)

The Lesser Black-backed Gull is found on seacliffs, shingle beaches, open moorland and mosses away from the sea, flat-topped islands and rocky areas near the sea. More rarely it will breed on rooftops in seaside towns. It normally breeds in colonies, which may be very large, but single nests occur. The nest is a hollow, well lined with dry grass or other available plant material. Incubation and care of the young is shared by both parents. It has a varied diet including fish, crustaceans, worms, insects, small mammals, eggs and nestlings of other birds, grain and all manner of refuse on the tideline or at rubbish tips.

It is predominantly migratory, entirely so in the north. It winters in small numbers in western Europe, but mainly in Mediterranean countries and off the coast of North Africa. Increasing numbers winter in southern Britain, feeding at rubbish tips and roosting on inland waters.

Migration: Departs breeding areas from August to October, returning in March—May.

Length:	53–56 cm
Wing length:	41–45 cm
Weight:	1000 g
Voice:	Barking or laughing calls, 'kyow', 'akakakak', like Herring Gull, but lower-pitched
Breeding period:	End of April, June, 1 brood per year. Replacement clutch possible
Size of clutch:	3 (1–2) eggs
Colour of eggs:	Light olive to rusty brown, with dark spots and blotches
Size of eggs:	68 × 47 mm
Incubation:	25–27 days, beginning before final egg
Fledging period:	Nidicolous; able to fly at ca 4–5 weeks

Scandinavian race (Ki)

Scandinavian race, Baltic Sea (Pl)

Amrum, June 1968 (Qu)

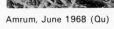

(left) West-European race, Amrum, North Sea, June 1968 (Qu)

Herring Gull (Larus argentatus)

The Herring Gull is widely distributed on the coasts and some inland areas of Europe. It breeds on seacliffs, particularly with grassy slopes, sandy or marshy areas, shingle banks, margins of freshwater lakes and mosses as well as on roofs of buildings in some areas. It is normally found in large colonies though single nests occur. The nest is a large accumulation of dry grass, seaweed or other plant material, though sometimes it uses mere scrapes with little additional material. Incubation and care of the young is shared by the parents.

It is omnivorous, taking fish, carrion, worms, insects, crustaceans and molluscs, eggs and nestlings, small mammals and all types of refuse. Inland it will take grain and other seeds. It lives in close association with man in many areas, frequenting harbours, rubbish tips and agricultural land at ploughing time and it follows fishing boats.

It winters throughout western Europe, the Mediterranean and North Africa. Many birds are resident but those from the north and east of the range tend to move south-west to winter. It occurs commonly inland as well as on the coast and is a common sight at rubbish tips.

Migration: Northern and eastern birds arrive in October–November, returning in March–April.

Length:	56–66 cm
Wing length:	41–47 cm
Weight:	1100 g
Voice:	Series of calls, 'kee-ow kee-ow' at nest; 'how-how', etc.
Breeding period:	End of April, June, 1 brood per year. Replacement clutch possible
Size of clutch:	3 (2) eggs
Colour of eggs:	Light greenish to olive-brown, with dark spots and patches
Size of eggs:	71 × 49 mm
Incubation:	25–27 days, beginning from first egg
Fledging period:	Nidicolous; independent at 8 weeks

Ad., Wales, May 1975 (Na)

(left) (L.a. cachinnans), Anatolia, Turkey, 25.5.1974 (Li)

Juv., Northern Greece, 20.6.1976 (Li)

Anatolia, 25.5.1974 (Li)

Common Gull (Larus canus)

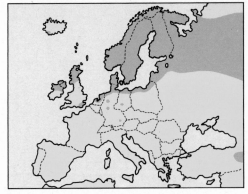

Common Gulls frequent moorland and mosses, hillsides near the sea, islands in lakes or offshore, shingle banks and, exceptionally, trees. The nests, which are usually in small colonies, are built of dry grass, heather and other plant material. Both parents take part in incubation and rearing the young.

Food includes insects, earthworms, grain and seeds, carrion, eggs and nestlings of other birds and small mammals. In coastal areas fish, molluscs and crustaceans form a large part of the diet.

The species winters in western Europe and the Mediterranean, though not in North Africa. Some birds are largely resident, moving from inland breeding sites to arable land or the coast. More northern and easterly populations move south-west to winter. Though frequent on the coast, it is also common in inland areas, feeding in flooded fields, ploughed land or at rubbish tips.

Migration: Autumn movements mainly August—October, with return in February—April.

Length:	41 cm
Wing length:	35 cm
Weight:	350 g
Voice:	Screaming 'kee-yah, kee-yah, kee-kee', like Herring Gull but shriller
Breeding period:	End of April, mid-May, 1 brood per year. Replacement clutch possible
Size of clutch:	3 (1–4) eggs
Colour of eggs:	Sandy, pale olive to rusty brown, with dark spots and blots
Size of eggs:	58 × 41 mm
Incubation:	22–28 days, beg. from complete clutch
Fledging period:	Nidicolous; able to fly at ca 5 weeks

'inter adult with Black-headed Gulls, Bavaria, 2.1977 (Li)
ft) Rundø, Norway, 1974 (Mo)

Chick, Amrum, North Sea, July 1975 (Qu)

Rundø, 1974 (Mo)

Slender-billed Gull (Larus genei)

In Europe this species is confined to the Mediterranean region. It frequents brackish and freshwater lagoons, deltas and river valleys, and offshore islands. It nests in colonies often in association with Gull-billed Terns and Black-headed or Mediterranean Gulls. The nest is a hollow in sand or mud, lined with plant matter and ringed by droppings. The nests may be very close together. Incubation and care of the young is probably by both sexes. It feeds on small fish, insects, worms and other animal matter.

It is resident in some areas but migratory in others; wintering birds are found on the coast of North Africa, and parts of the Middle East as well as in the Mediterranean. Its movements are not fully understood. Large numbers are found in the Persian Gulf but it is not known if European birds are involved.

Migration: Dispersal takes place from August to October, birds returning to breeding areas in April—May.

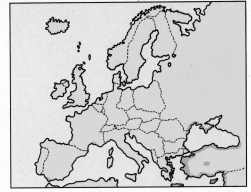

Length:	43 cm
Wing length:	31–32 cm
Weight:	280 g
Voice:	Nasal calls, 'kree-yang' or 'kak-kak'
Breeding period:	Beginning of May, June, 1 brood per year. Replacement clutch possible
Size of clutch:	2–3 (1) eggs
Colour of eggs:	Cream to bluish white, with dark spots and patches
Size of eggs:	56 × 39 mm
Incubation:	22–24 days, beg. from complete clutch
Fledging period:	Nidicolous; able to fly at 5–6 weeks

fending the nesting place, Anatolia, 10.6.1973 (Li)

eft) Colony, Central Anatolia, Turkey, 3.6.1974 (Pf)

Anatolia, 5.6.1974 (Pf)

Anatolia, 2.6.1974 (Li)

297

Mediterranean Gull

(Larus melanocephalus)

Though the eastern Mediterranean and Black Sea areas are the stronghold of this species, it also breeds in very small numbers in eastern Europe, the Netherlands and recently in Britain. It typically frequents salt-marshes and islands in shallow lakes or saline lagoons. Outside its main range it tends to associate with colonies of Black-headed Gulls. The nest is a shallow cup lined with plant-stems, grass and feathers. Both parents share incubation and care of the young. Birds in sub-adult plumage take part in display and may breed successfully. Hybrids are known between this species and Black-headed Gull. Information on diet is lacking but it is probably similar to that of the Slender-billed and Black-headed Gulls. The species is a partial migrant, wintering on the coasts of southern England, the Atlantic coast of France and North Africa as well as in the Mediterranean. The timing and routes of migration are not fully understood.

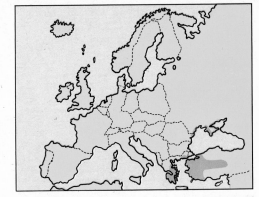

Length:	40 cm
Wing length:	32 cm
Weight:	250 g
Voice:	'Kyaau', 'kek-ke-ke'
Breeding period:	End of May, June, 1 brood per year. Replacement clutch possible
Size of clutch:	3 (2) eggs
Colour of eggs:	Cream to brownish, with dark patches and spots
Size of eggs:	54 × 38 mm
Incubation:	*ca* 24 days, beg. from complete clutch
Fledging period:	Nidicolous; able to fly at 5–6 weeks

Anatolia, 2.6.1974 (Li)

Anatolia, 5.6.1974 (Pf)

Anatolia, 2.6.1974 (Li)

ft) Courtship between ad. and imm. birds, Anatolia, Turkey, 2.6.1974 (Li)

Black-headed Gull (Larus ridibundus)

The Black-headed Gull is the commonest and most widespread gull over most of Europe. The species is at home in coastal salt-marsh, dunes, the reedy margins of inland waters, moorland pools and grassy islands in lakes. It nests in colonies of a few to many thousands of pairs, often in association with terns. The nest is a scrape built up with varying amounts of reed stems, grass and other plant material, mainly by the ♂. Both parents share in incubation and rearing the young.

The diet is very varied depending upon the habitat, but includes earth-worms, insects, small fish, seeds, grain, fruit and refuse at rubbish tips and sewage outfalls.

The species winters in western Europe, North Africa, the Mediterranean and the Middle East. Northern and eastern populations are the most migratory; elsewhere birds disperse from the breeding colonies to winter on the coast or arable land. The Black-headed Gull is a successful, opportunist bird and has expanded its range considerably in the north of Europe.

Migration: Dispersal from breeding colonies in July—August, returning in March—May.

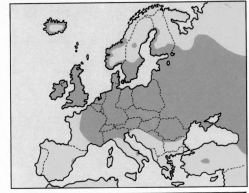

Length:	38 cm
Wing length:	30 cm
Weight:	250 g
Voice:	Screaming 'kree-aah', 'kak-kak'
Breeding period:	May, June, 1 brood per year. Replacement clutch possible
Size of clutch:	3 (2—6) eggs
Colour of eggs:	Variable, from pale blue or olive to rusty brown, with dark patches and scrawls
Size of eggs:	52 × 37 mm
Incubation:	21—27 days, beginning with first egg
Fledging period:	Nidicolous; able to fly at 5—6 weeks

...d., Bavaria, West Germany, 6.1.1977 (Pf)

...eft) Central Anatolia, Turkey, 6.6.1974 (Pf)

Imm., Bavaria, 6.1.1977 (Pf)

Nest with regurgitated cherry-stones, Neusiedler See, Austria, 1961 (Li)

301

Kittiwake (Rissa tridactyla)

The Kittiwake is the most oceanic of the European breeding gulls. It nests on ledges of seacliffs and sometimes on buildings in seaside towns. It nests in colonies, often in company with other cliff-nesting seabirds. The nest is a well-constructed cup of grass, mud and seaweed built on a projection or irregularity of rock. Incubation and care of the young is shared by both parents. The diet includes fish, mainly sand-eels in some areas, as well as insects, crustaceans, worms and animal plankton. Birds often follow fishing boats taking scraps of offal, or haunt fishing ports scavenging scraps.

In winter Kittiwakes are largely pelagic, wintering across the Atlantic and in the North Sea and western Mediterranean. It is very rare inland. It is social throughout the year, large flocks being seen collecting nest material, bathing in freshwater pools and at feeding areas.

Migration: Dispersal from breeding colonies in August—September, returning in March—April.

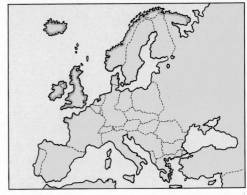

Length:	41 cm
Wing length:	31 cm
Weight:	420 g
Voice:	Very noisy at nesting place: 'ka-ka-ka', 'kitti-wake'
Breeding period:	End of May, June, 1 brood per year. Replacement clutch possible
Size of clutch:	2 (1–3) eggs
Colour of eggs:	Cream to light brown, with fine dark patches or dots
Size of eggs:	56 × 41 mm
Incubation:	22–24 days, beg. from complete clutch
Fledging period:	Nidicolous; able to fly at 5–6 weeks

oula, Shetland, May 1974 (Zi)
'eft) Ad. and young birds (FI)

Rundø, Norway, 28.6.1966 (Sy)

Chick in nest, Rundø, June 1974 (Par)

303

Black Tern (Chlidonias niger)

Black Terns are found on shallow fresh or brackish waters, usually with reedy or swampy vegetation. It breeds in colonies, the nests usually sited on floating vegetation or on firm ground in emergent vegetation. Sometimes the nest is built up in the water from reeds and other aquatic plants. Both sexes share in incubation and rearing the young, the ♀ taking the larger share of incubation. The diet consists mainly of insects and their larvae, as well as small fish and other aquatic animals. The food is taken in the air or picked from the surface of the water, the species often feeding in groups. The breeding distribution of the species in Europe is rather erratic, with many instances of birds nesting outside the normal range. It is entirely migratory, wintering mostly on the coasts of tropical Africa and perhaps inland also.

Migration: Autumn movements from late July to October, returning in April—June.

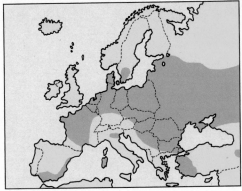

Length:	24 cm
Wing length:	21 cm
Weight:	65 g
Voice:	Rarely heard: 'kik-kik', 'krrrr'
Breeding period:	May, June, 1 brood per year. Replacement clutch possible
Size of clutch:	3 (2–4) eggs
Colour of eggs:	Mud-coloured to olive-brown, irregular dark brown patches
Size of eggs:	34 × 25 mm
Incubation:	14–18 days, beg. from complete clutch
Fledging period:	Nidicolous; remaining ca 2 weeks in nest. Fledged at about 4 weeks

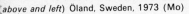
(*above and left*) Öland, Sweden, 1973 (Mo)

Öland, 1973 (Mo)

305

Whiskered Tern (Chlidonias hybrida)

The Whiskered Tern has a more southerly distribution than the Black Tern, but, like that species, its breeding colonies are erratic and it often nests outside its normal range. It frequents marshes and fresh or brackish waters with a good amount of surface vegetation. The nest is often a fragile structure of reed stems and other plant material floating amongst surface plants; sometimes it is attached to rushes or other plants. Incubation is by both sexes, but mostly by the ♀; both parents share in rearing the young. The whiskered Tern feeds by picking objects from the surface of the water, dipping down from a shallow flight. It takes mostly small fish and other aquatic animals, as well as insects and their larvae.

The species is entirely migratory in Europe, wintering in the Nile delta and in tropical Africa. Locusts make up much of the diet in East Africa.

Migration: Autumn movements in September—October, returning in late April and May.

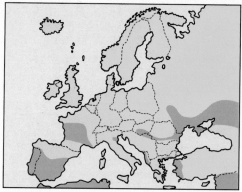

Length:	25 cm
Wing length:	24 cm
Weight:	90 g
Voice:	Screaming 'keeik', 'kyo' or 'shree-aah'
Breeding period:	End of April, June, 1 brood per year. Replacement clutch possible
Size of clutch:	3 (2–4) eggs
Colour of eggs:	Light green to brownish, with dark spots and patches
Size of eggs:	39 × 28 mm
Incubation:	20–22 days, beg. from complete clutch
Fledging period:	Nidicolous; fledged at ca 4 weeks

rthern Greece, 22.5.1972 (Li)

Juv., Macedonia, Greece, 8.7.1977 (Sy)

Northern Greece, 22.5.1972 (Li)

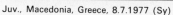

t) ♂ presenting ♀ with fish, Northern Greece, 22.5.1972 (Li)

Gull-billed Tern (Gelochelidon nilotica)

The Gull-billed Tern is found chiefly on the shores of saline lagoons, shallow lakes, dunes and sandflats. It has a very discontinuous distribution in Europe and sometimes breeds outside its normal range, exceptionally in Britain. It usually nests in colonies, the nest being a shallow scrape in soft sand or earth sparsely lined with plant materials. Incubation and care of the young is shared by both parents. It takes a variety of food including small mammals, large insects, earthworms, eggs and nestlings of other birds, small reptiles and amphibians. It will also take fish and aquatic animals to a lesser extent. It flies low over the ground in search of food, as well as fishing in shallow water.

The species is entirely migratory in Europe, wintering in a band across tropical Africa, occurring inland as well as on the coast.

Migration: Autumn movements in August to early October, with return in spring from late March to May.

Length:	39 cm
Wing length:	32 cm
Weight:	200 g
Voice:	Loud and harsh 'ka-huk-ka-huk', 'kaahk'
Breeding period:	Mid-May, June, 1 brood per year. Replacement clutch possible
Size of clutch:	3 (2–5) eggs
Colour of eggs:	Cream to brownish, with dark spots and patches
Size of eggs:	49 × 35 mm
Incubation:	22–23 days, beg. from complete clutch
Fledging period:	Nidicolous; able to fly at 4–5 weeks

entral Anatolia, 6.6.1974 (Pf)

eft) Colony of Gull-billed Terns, Anatolia, Turkey, 10.6.1973 (Li)

Ad. with chicks, Anatolia, 10.6.1973 (Li)

Anatolia, June 1973 (Li)

Caspian Tern (Sterna caspia)

The Caspian Tern inhabits sandy or shingle beaches on the coast or offshore islands. In the south-east of its range it is also found on inland lakes. It nests in colonies which may be very large, the eggs being laid in a shallow scrape which is usually unlined. Both parents share incubation and care of the young. The Caspian Tern is a large, powerful bird. It feeds mainly on fish obtained by plunge-diving, but will also take large insects and the eggs and young of other birds.

European birds are migratory; a few overwinter in the southern Mediterranean and North-African coasts but most migrate to tropical Africa, where they winter along the coast and on inland lakes.

Migration: Birds leave the breeding colonies from late July with passage continuing to October. They return in April—May, even June in the north.

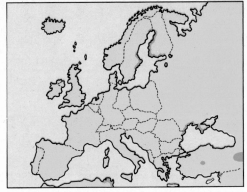

Length:	53 cm
Wing length:	42 cm
Weight:	500 g
Voice:	A hoarse 'kaah-kaah' and 'kuk-kuk-kuk' resembling call of Heron
Breeding period:	May, June, 1 brood per year. Replacement clutch possible
Size of clutch:	2—3 eggs
Colour of eggs:	Light sandy colour, with small dark spots and patches
Size of eggs:	64 × 45 mm
Incubation:	20—23 days, beginning from first egg
Fledging period:	Nidicolous; able to fly at 3—4 weeks

Courtship, ♂ right, Anatolia, 28.5.1974 (Li)

(left) Colony of Caspian Terns, Anatolia, Turkey, 28.5.1974 (Li)

Copulation, Anatolia, 28.5.1974 (Li)

Anatolia, 28.5.1974 (Li)

Common Tern (Sterna hirundo)

The Common Tern is the commonest and most widespread tern in Europe. It breeds on shingle or sandbanks on the coast or in large rivers and lakes, offshore islands, lagoons, open heath or moorland near the coast and marshy areas in inland waters. They are essentially gregarious birds, often nesting in large colonies, sometimes in association with other Terns or Gulls. The nest is generally a shallow scrape with little or no lining, but in marshy areas it may be built up with plant material. Incubation is shared by both parents but mostly by the ♀; both sexes tend the young. The localities of colonies often change dramatically from year to year and at times breeding success is very low, with losses of 80 per cent or more. The diet is mainly small fish, aquatic invertebrates, insects and crustaceans.

European birds are entirely migratory, wintering on tropical coasts, mainly off West and South Africa. They are remarkable long-range migrants; a British-ringed bird has been recovered in Australia.

Migration: Leaves breeding colonies in late July and August and most have left European waters by November. They return in late March to May.

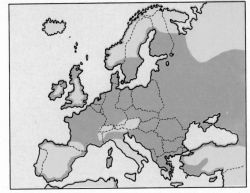

Length:	35 cm
Wing length:	27 cm
Weight:	150 g
Voice:	Screaming 'kree-aar', 'kik-kik-kik'; very noisy
Breeding period:	End of May, June, 1 brood per year. Replacement clutch possible
Size of clutch:	3 (2–4) eggs
Colour of eggs:	Variable sandy to olive-brown, with dark patches
Size of eggs:	41 × 30 mm
Incubation:	20–23 days, beginning from first egg
Fledging period:	Nidicolous; able to fly at 4 weeks

avaria, West Germany, 1963 (Li)

eft) Northern Greece, 18.5.1972 (Li)

Juv. Common Tern, Bavaria (Kacher)

Bavaria, June 1960 (Pf)

Arctic Tern (Sterna paradisaea)

The Arctic Tern has a more northerly distribution than the Common Tern and is generally more coastal than that species. It breeds in colonies, sometimes in association with other Terns, on shingle banks, rocky off-shore islands, short coastal turf or moorland areas with sparse vegetation, and marshy areas in the tundra. The nest is generally a scrape with little or no lining of plant material and is made by the ♀. Both sexes incubate and tend the young. The Arctic Tern is often aggressive in defence of its nest site and will strike intruders, including humans. It feeds mainly on small fish, often sand-eels, crustaceans and a variety of insects particularly when breeding inland.

The Arctic Tern is entirely migratory, performing one of the longest migratory journeys of any bird. It winters at sea off the coasts of southern Africa and the southern oceans as far south as the Antarctic. In winter it feeds mainly on 'krill' as well as small fish.

Migration: It leaves the breeding colonies from late July, with movements continuing into October. Return passage is in April—May or June in the north.

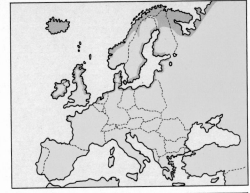

Length:	38 cm
Wing length:	26—28 cm
Weight:	110 g
Voice:	A rising 'kee kee', 'kirr-kirr' or 'kree-aah'
Breeding period:	End of April to June, 1 brood per year. Replacement clutch possible
Size of clutch:	2 (1—3) eggs
Colour of eggs:	Whitish to brown or olive, with dark patches
Size of eggs:	40 × 29 mm
Incubation:	20—22 days, beginning from first egg
Fledging period:	Nidicolous; able to fly at 3—4 weeks

Lower Saxony, West Germany (We)

(left) Changing places on the nest, Öland, Sweden, 1973 (Mo)

Öland, May 1973 (Par)

Sweden, June 1974 (Mo)

Little Tern (Sterna albifrons)

The Little Tern has a very wide distribution, occurring both inland and on the coast in the various parts of its range. It breeds in small colonies on sand or shingle banks on the coast or dry areas along large rivers and estuaries. The nest is a shallow scrape sometimes lined with small pebbles, shell fragments or plant material, and is built by the ♀. Incubation and care of the young is shared by both parents.

It feeds on small aquatic animals, mainly fish, crustaceans and marine worms, and insects and their larvae when breeding inland. It obtains its food by vertical plunge-diving.

The European population is migratory, wintering mainly on the coasts of tropical West Africa. It has decreased markedly over much of its north European range and is endangered in many areas. Disturbance of breeding colonies by humans is a major factor in its decline.

Migration: Departs breeding colonies from July, migration continuing to October. Return passage is mainly in April and May.

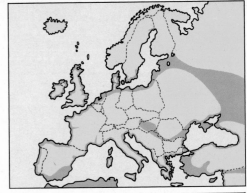

Length:	23 cm
Wing length:	17 cm
Weight:	50 g
Voice:	Shrill, hard series of calls: 'kik-kik', 'kyik' and 'kirri-kirri-kirri'
Breeding period:	Mid-May, June, 1 brood per year. Replacement clutch possible
Size of clutch:	2–3 eggs
Colour of eggs:	Sandy to rust-brown, with dark patches
Size of eggs:	33 × 24 mm
Incubation:	20–22 days, beginning from second egg
Fledging period:	Nidicolous; able to fly from 15 to 17 days

Northern Greece, May 1976 (Zei)

(left) ♂ feeding ♀ with fish, Northern Greece, 19.5.1972 (Li)

Young bird, Northern Greece, May 1976 (Zei)

Northern Greece, 19.5.1972 (Li)

Sandwich Tern (Sterna sandvicensis)

In Europe the Sandwich Tern has a coastal distribution; it occurs in dunes, sandy or shingle beaches and low islands with sparse vegetation. It breeds in colonies, often in association with Black-headed Gulls or other Terns. The nest is a shallow hollow often lined with plant debris. Both birds take part in incubation and care of the young. It feeds mainly on marine fish which it obtains by fierce plunge-diving, sand-eels often making up the bulk of the diet. Other food includes marine invertebrates such as crustaceans.

The European population is migratory, wintering mainly off the coast of West Africa but also in North-African waters and parts of the Mediterranean.

Migration: Prolonged autumn movements from mid-July to October, returning in March to May.

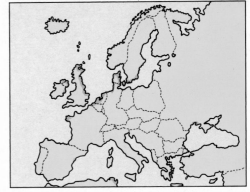

Length:	41 cm
Wing length:	31 cm
Weight:	250 g
Voice:	Screaming and hoarse cries, 'kirrick' or 'ke-rake, ke-rake'
Breeding period:	End of April, May, 1 brood per year. Replacement clutch possible
Size of clutch:	2 (1–3) eggs
Colour of eggs:	Cream to sandy brown, with dark spots and blotches
Size of eggs:	51 × 36 mm
Incubation:	22–24 days, beginning before last egg
Fledging period:	Nidicolous; leaving the nest at 10 days, able to fly at about 35 days

Trischen, 26.5.1968 (Bö)

Colony on Norderoog, North Sea, June 1960 (Qu)

Norderoog, June 1960 (Qu)

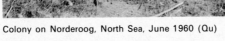

left) Ad. with juv. among Common Terns, Holland (Wo)

Razorbill (Alca torda)

The Razorbill breeds exclusively on seacoasts. It nests in crevices in cliffs, among boulders at the foot of cliffs, in caves and sometimes on open rock-ledges. They will often associate with Guillemots on the breeding ledges. Displaying birds have a 'butterfly' aerial display, flying with slow, deliberate wingbeats. No nest is built, the single egg being laid on the bare rock. In boulder-beach sites a few small pebbles may be gathered together to form the nest site. Incubation and care of the chick is shared by both parents, the off-duty bird feeding at sea whilst the other broods. Razorbills feed entirely at sea. The main diet is small fish, particularly sand-eels and sprats; small numbers of crustaceans and some molluscs are also taken. Food is obtained by surface-diving and pursuing prey underwater.

Razorbills are migratory, wintering at sea mainly in the Atlantic and North Seas. Some birds move as far south as the coasts of Iberia and North Africa and a few enter the Mediterranean.

Migration: Departs breeding colonies in late July to August, returning in January—February in the south, March—April in the north.

Length:	40 cm
Wing length:	21 cm
Weight:	800 g
Voice:	Deep creaking calls, 'karrr' or 'arrr'
Breeding period:	Beginning of May, June, 1 brood per year. Replacement clutch possible
Size of clutch:	1 (2) eggs
Colour of eggs:	Variable, white to sandy or reddish brown. Dark patches and streaks
Size of eggs:	73 × 47 mm
Incubation:	34—39 days
Fledging period:	Nidicolous; leaving the cliff after *ca* 18 days to swim accompanied by parents

hanging places on the nest, Rundø, 26.6.1966 (Sy)

eft) Rundø, Norway, 1974 (Mo)

Rundø, 10.7.1966 (Sy)

Röst Island, Norway (Par)

Guillemot (Uria aalge)

Guillemots breed in dense colonies on seacliff ledges, flat-topped stacks, caves and crevices. The colonies are often so dense that incubating birds touch each other. No nest is built, the egg being laid on the bare rock, as its pyriform shape helps to stop it rolling off. Incubation is by both parents as is the care of the chick. The food is mainly fish, particularly sand-eels and sprats, and is obtained by surface-diving and pursuing the prey underwater. Some crustaceans and molluscs are also taken. The young leave the nest before they are able to fly, jumping into the sea, often at night when there is less risk from predators.

Guillemots winter at sea, mostly in the Atlantic and North Sea. They have complicated movements with birds from certain colonies wintering in specific areas; birds from the north of Scotland move mainly to Scandinavian coasts.

Migration: Dispersive, leaving the breeding colonies from July and returning (adults only) for short periods from October onwards, and regularly from February or March.

A plumage morph, the 'bridled' Guillemot with a white eye-ring and stripe, occurs among normal plumage birds, mostly in the north.

Length:	40 cm
Wing length:	21 cm
Weight:	1000 g
Voice:	Deep hoarse 'arrr' or 'ohrrr'
Breeding period:	Mid-May, June, 1 brood per year. Replacement clutch possible
Size of clutch:	1 egg
Colour of egg:	Very variable. White, yellow, green, blue or reddish brown base with dark patches, scrawls or lines; may also be plain
Size of egg:	82 × 50 mm
Incubation:	32–34 days
Fledging period:	Nidicolous; juvenile leaves the cliffs at 18–25 days and swims in open water accompanied by parents

Bridled Guillemot, Foula, June 1974 (Zi)

(left) Ad. with juv., Foula, Shetland, June 1974 (Zi)

Non-breeding plumage, Amrum, North Sea, October 1961 (Qu)

Foula, May 1974 (Zi)

323

Black Guillemot or Tystie

(Cepphus grylle)

The Tystie has a more northerly distribution than the other European auks. It breeds on rocky coasts in boulder beaches, crevices and caves, old walls close to the sea and, more rarely, in holes in earth banks or turf. No nest is made but sites in boulder beaches may be lined with small stones or other debris. Colonies are generally small, and single nests are common. Both sexes share in incubation and care of the young. There is a communal display with several pairs calling and following each other, often in line-formation on the sea near to the nest-sites. The diet is mainly small fish, particularly Butterfish, crustacea and molluscs. It feeds mostly in shallow, inshore waters in contrast to the other auks. The species is largely resident, birds remaining close to the nesting areas throughout the year. Some movement of young birds may take place, though it is rarely found south of its breeding range.

Length:	34 cm
Wing length:	17 cm
Weight:	500 g
Voice:	A piping, 'sphee-ee-ee'
Breeding period:	May–June, 1 brood per year. Replacement clutch possible
Size of clutch:	2 (1–3) eggs
Colour of eggs:	Whitish to blue-green with grey and brown flecks
Size of eggs:	58 × 40 mm
Incubation:	about 29 days
Fledging period:	Nidicolous; leaving the 'nest' after 34–36 days

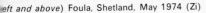
(left and above) Foula, Shetland, May 1974 (Zi)

Chick removed from nest, Rundø, Norway, July 1976 (Di)

Puffin (Fratercula arctica)

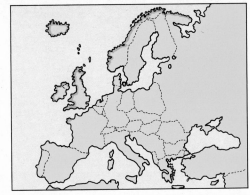

Puffins live on sea-coasts, often in vast colonies, and they nest in burrows in turf slopes, or on tops of cliffs and stacks as well as in rock crevices and among boulders. The burrows are excavated by the parents using their feet, which have sharp claws. Sometimes burrows of rabbits or Manx Shearwater are used. The nest-chamber is lined with a little plant material and feathers. Both sexes incubate and feed the chick. Food is mainly fish, particularly sand-eels and sprats. Several fish are often held crosswise in the beak and brought back to feed the chick.

The single chick is deserted at about six weeks and left to fend for itself. It usually leaves the burrow at night to avoid predators.

Outside the breeding season Puffins are pelagic, wandering the Atlantic and the North Sea. Some move to the coasts of Iberia and into the western Mediterranean, others may move north to Greenland or North America. The true winter distribution is not fully known.

Migration: Breeding colonies are deserted from August to March or April.

Length:	30 cm
Wing length:	16 cm
Weight:	400 g
Voice:	Hoarse grating sounds, 'arrr' or 'orrr' and 'rrro'
Breeding period:	April to May, 1 brood per year. Replacement clutch possible
Size of clutch:	1 (2) eggs
Colour of eggs:	White, sometimes with faint brown patches
Size of eggs:	61 × 42 mm
Incubation:	40–43 days
Fledging period:	Nidicolous; independent at ca 6 weeks

...undø, 27.6.1966 (Sy)

...eft) Rundø, Norway, 1974 (Mo)

Juv. removed from nest, Rundø, 9.7.1966 (Sy)

Rundø, 18.6.1966 (Sy)

Species breeding regularly in Europe but not
included in Vol. 1, or treated summarily:

Great Northern Diver	*Gavia immer*
Slavonian Grebe	*Podiceps auritus*
Cory's Shearwater	*Calonectris diomedea*
Manx Shearwater	*Puffinus puffinus*
Storm Petrel	*Hydrobates pelagicus*
Leach's Petrel	*Oceanodroma leucorhoa*
Pygmy Cormorant	*Phalacrocorax pygmeus*
Cattle Egret	*Bubulcus ibis*
Egyptian Goose	*Alopochen aegyptiacus*
Mandarin	*Aix galericulata*
Marbled Duck	*Marmaronetta angustirostris*
Harlequin Duck	*Histrionicus histrionicus*
Barrow's Goldeneye	*Bucephala islandica*
Ruddy Duck	*Oxyura jamaicensis*
White-headed Duck	*Oxyura leucocephala*
Spotted Eagle	*Aquila clanga*
Bonelli's Eagle	*Hieraaetus fasciatus*
Black-winged Kite	*Elanus caeruleus*
Pallid Harrier	*Circus macrourus*
Merlin	*Falco columbarius*
Red-footed Falcon	*Falco vespertinus*
Lanner	*Falco biarmicus*
Gyrfalcon	*Falco rusticolus*
Chukar	*Alectoris chukar*
Red-legged Partridge	*Alectoris rufa*
Barbary Partridge	*Alectoris barbara*
Golden Pheasant	*Chrysolophus pictus*
Lady Amherst's Pheasant	*C. amherstiae*
Andalusian Hemipode	*Turnix sylvatica*
Little Crake	*Porzana parva*
Baillon's Crake	*Porzana pusilla*
Corncrake	*Crex crex*
Purple Gallinule	*Porphyrio porphyrio*
Crested Coot	*Fulica cristata*
Broad-billed Sandpiper	*Limicola falcinellus*
Marsh Sandpiper	*Tringa stagnatilis*
Terek Sandpiper	*Xenus cinereus*
Grey Phalarope	*Phalaropus fulicarius*
Little Gull	*Larus minutus*
Audouin's Gull	*Larus audouinii*
Glaucous Gull	*Larus hyperboreus*
White-winged Black Tern	*Chlidonias leucopterus*
Roseate Tern	*Sterna dougallii*
Brunnich's Guillemot	*Uria lomvia*
Little Auk	*Alle alle*

Summary of Contents

Volume II

Pterocliformes
Pteroclidae—Sandgrouse

Columbiformes
Columbidae—Pigeons and Doves

Cuculiformes
Cuculidae—Cuckoos

Strigiformes
Tytonidae—Barn Owl
Strigidae—Owls

Caprimulgiformes
Caprimulgidae—Nightjars

Apodiformes
Apodidae—Swifts

Coraciiformes
Alcedinidae—Kingfishers
Meropidae—Bee-Eaters
Coraciidae—Rollers
Upupidae—Hoopoes

Piciformes
Picidae—Woodpeckers

Passeriformes
Alaudidae—Larks
Hirundinidae—Swallows and Martins
Motacillidae—Pipits and Wagtails
Laniidae—Shrikes
Bombycillidae—Waxwings
Cinclidae—Dippers
Troglodytidae—Wrens
Prunellidae—Accentors
Sylviidae—Warblers
Muscicapidae—Flycatchers
Timaliidae—Bearded Tits

Aegithalidae—Long-tailed Tits
Remizidae—Penduline Tits
Paridae—Tits
Sittidae—Nuthatches
Tichodromidae—Wall-creepers
Certhiidae—Tree-creepers
Emberizidae—Buntings
Fringillidae—Finches
Passeridae—Sparrows
Sturnidae—Starlings
Oriolidae—Orioles
Corvidae—Crows, Magpies,
  Jays, etc.

Distribution Maps

The areas shaded green indicate the breeding territory of the species concerned. This does not imply that the bird may be found breeding everywhere within the area indicated. This is always dependent on a suitable biotope (habitat). To facilitate identification of the areas, national boundaries have been marked. It has not been possible to take account of individual breeding spots outside the main breeding areas, owing to the small size of the maps. In any case such breeding places are generally used very irregularly and may die out at any time. On some maps two species have had to be included, in which case the breeding area of the second species has been indicated by black dots.

Distribution maps: Manfred Pforr

Symbols and Abbreviations

The following abbreviations and symbols have been used in the text:

Ad. (adult) = sexually mature bird, adult plumage
Imm. (immature) = not in full adult plumage, sexually immature
Juv. (juvenile) = juvenile plumage
BP = Breeding plumage
NBP = Non-breeding plumage
♂ = male, ♀ = female

The Photographs

The abbreviations in brackets after the picture-captions represent the names of the photographers who have supplied often irreplaceable material for reproduction in *The Breeding Birds of Europe*. Addresses are in West Germany except where otherwise indicated.

(Dr A)	Dr H. Aschenbrenner, Neukirchen/Hl. Blut		(Par)	Helmut Partsch, Wemding
(Ar)	Hansgeorg Arndt, Lübeck		(Pf)	Manfred Pforr, Moosburg
(Be)	Albrecht Belz, Erndtebrück		(Pl)	Alfons Plucinski, Goslar
(Bö)	Edgar Böhme, Neu Wulmstorf		(Qu)	Georg Quedens, Norddorf/Amrum Island
(Di)	Jürgen Diedrich, Ronnenberg 1		(Rei)	Fred Reinwarth, Dachau
(Fe)	Walter Fendrich, Vienna, Austria		(Sa)	Gerhard Sauer, Neunkirchen-Altenseelbach
(Fl)	Walter Fleuster, Bochum		(Sch)	Otmar Scharbert, Bürgstadt
(O. v. F.)	Prof. Otto von Frisch, Braunschweig		(Schu)	Werner Schubert, Sindelfingen
(Gé)	Benny Génsbøl, Tisvilde, Denmark		(Se)	Walter Sedlmeier, Landshut
(Gl)	Hans Glader, Rhede		(Si)	Norbert Sischka, Germersheim 2
(Ka)	Jochen Kankel, Munich 80		(Sou)	Rudolf Souilljee, Bocholt-Biemenhorst
(Kacher)	Hermann Kacher, Seewiesen		(St)	Herfried Steidl, Weiden/Almensbach
(Ki)	Klaus Kirchner, Henstedt-Ulzburg		(Sy)	Günter Synatzschke, Rotenburg/Wümme
(Kü)	Karl Kühnel, Dietramszell		(Tö)	Konrad Tönges, Lahntal-Grossfelden
(Li)	Alfred Limbrunner, Dachau		(Wa)	Dr Klaus Warncke, Dachau
(Ma)	Reinhard Mache, Stuttgart 1		(We)	Jürgen Weber, Hannover 72
(Mak)	Dr Wolfgang Makatsch, Bautzen		(Willy)	Josef Willy, Munich 70
(Mey)	Dr Bernd Ulrich Meyburg, Berlin 33		(Wi)	Richard Wismath, Füssen
(Mö)	Reiner Mönig, Wuppertal 2		(Wö)	Wöhler, Ronnenberg 1
(Mo)	Günter Moosrainer, Dachau		(Wo)	Konrad Wothe, Munich 81
(Na)	Wolfgang Nagel, Stuttgart		(Zi)	Günter Ziesler, Munich 82
(Nek)	Wilhelm Nekvasil, Vienna, Austria		(Zei)	Peter Zeiniger, Munich 81

Index
of English
Bird Names

Index
of Scientific Bird Names